NOBODY'S CHILD

by Marie Balter and Richard Katz

"Her extraordinary past imitates nineteenth-century literature, Jane Eyre, say, or David Copperfield."

The New York Times

"One amazing story, with symptoms captured to a fare-thee-well, and an upbeat ending that can't fail to move the reader."

Kirkus Reviews

"In the tradition of . . . *I Never Promised You a Rose Garden.*"
Carl Salzman, M.D.
Harvard Medical School

"If you've ever . . . felt that you couldn't go on, this is the book for you."

Father John Catoir
Director of The Christophers

"An amazing story of stamina, courage, and the will to live . . . . Highly recommended."

Booklist

"Here is one woman standing up to the dragon and winning."

Phil Donahue

ADDISON–WESLEY PUBLISHING COMPANY, INC.

READING, MASSACHUSETTS

DON MILLS, ONTARIO

SYDNEY   SINGAPORE   TOKYO   MADRID

MEXICO CITY   TAIPEI

NOBODY'S CHILD

Marie Balter and Richard Katz

A MERLOYD LAWRENCE BOOK

MENLO PARK, CALIFORNIA   NEW YORK

WOKINGHAM, ENGLAND   AMSTERDAM   BONN

SAN JUAN   PARIS   SEOUL   MILAN

This story is true to the best of our understanding. Certain names of persons and places have been changed to protect their identities.

Library of Congress Cataloging-in-Publication Data
Balter, Marie, 1930–
   [Sing no sad songs]
   Nobody's child / Marie Balter, Richard Katz.
     p. cm.
   Reprint, with new pref. Originally published: Sing no sad
songs. Massachusetts : Balter Institute, c1987.
   "A Merloyd Lawrence book."
   ISBN 0-201-57073-4
   ISBN 0-201-60816-2 (pbk.)
   1. Balter, Marie, 1930—Mental health. 2. Psychoses—
Patients—United States—Biography. I. Katz, Richard, 1937– .
II. Title.
RC512.B35   1991
616.89'0092—dc20
[B]   90-45537

Cover design by Stephen Gleason
Text design by Linda Koegel
Text photograph by Dorothy Littell
Set in 11-point Bembo by Camden Type 'n Graphics, Camden, ME

1 2 3 4 5 6 7 8 9-MW-95949392
Second printing, March 1991
First paperback printing, April 1992

To all who seek hope

Contents

Acknowledgments

•

To all those who have helped Marie along the way:

Mr. William Akers
Ms. Adele Anderson
Yitzak Bakal, Ph.D.
Mr. & Mrs. Bruce Balter
The late Joseph Balter
Mr. Anthony Barbara
The late Mr. & Mrs. Jack Barbara
Dr. & Mrs. Peter Barker & family
Roberta Brinker, R.N.
Sheldon Brown, Ph.D.
Linda Budd
William Budd
Lay Carmelites, Danvers Chapter
The late Margaret Christie
Mr. & Mrs. George Christo & family
The late Rosalie Ciarmitaro
Mother Mary Clarissa
Sherri Cohen
Ms. Lee Collier
Father Alan Crowley, O.C.D.
The late John DeSantis & family
Susan Duggan
Mr. & Mrs. David Eaton & family
The late Mother Eaton

Barbara Edell, R.N.
My Friends, "The Beach Court Gang"
Virginia Frontiero
The late Rose Godbout, R.N.
Ms. Thelma Grant
Mr. Donald Greenough
Ms. Rochelle Hale
Mr. & Mrs. Walter Jankowski & famil
Former Senator Jack King
Mr. David Kline
Dr. Constantine Kostas
Sr. Genevieve Kunkle, S.S.N.D.
Ruth Lord, M.D.
Mr. & Mrs. John Mahoney
Ms. Lois Mansfield
Lee McLaughlin, L.P.N.
The late Catherine Montagnino
Mr. & Mrs. Chester T. Morrison
Ms. Shirley Needham
Mr. & Mrs. David Norman
The late Edna O'Brien
Mr. James Oien
Ms. Mary Orlando
Sr. Mary Pauline

ix

Ms. Joan Rapp
Ms. Filomena Rodolosi & family
The late Lena Scuderi & family
The late Father Sephton
Howard E. Stone, Jr., M.D.

Ms. Ruth Tefferteller
Ms. Lori Turlo
Mr. & Mrs. Louis Turlo
Dorothy Vaitkunas, R.N.

To those who have helped make this book:
John Anderson, Calvin Barnes, Celeste Barnes, Peg Bowen, Cynthia Brehmer,
Cathy Jankowski, Phyllis Karas, Eber Hampton, Paul Jacoby, Merloyd
Lawrence, Carl Salzman, Freema Shapiro, Bruce Shatswell, Rick Weissbourd,
Ana Wexler, Bob Williamson, and especially Verna St. Denis.

And special thanks to Barbara Thompson, Marie's housemate, friend and work
colleague for her support and help.

Preface

RICHARD KATZ

Nearly all her life, Marie Balter has been coping with mental illness, first her own, and in recent years, that of others. Out of an office which serves more as a point of departure than a resting place, she works on community mental health programs around Boston and throughout the New England states. Many of her clients are past or present clients of Sutton State Hospital for the mentally ill, where Marie, now sixty, was confined for most of a twenty-year period in her early adult life.

Marie and I met at Harvard in 1982, when Marie was taking several courses with me while obtaining her master's degree. When we first talked, the distance between Sutton State Hospital and Harvard seemed short. Marie lives her life as an ordinary person, speaking with care and humility about the extraordinary journey which led her from the back ward of an institution for the mentally disturbed to the classroom of an institution for the intellectually elite.

Yet, now, as we get to know each other, and I learn more about the struggles which created that journey, the distance between Sutton State and Harvard seems vast. We can think of it as miraculous, especially given that Marie's sensitivity and talent were imprisoned in an often uncaring and even cruel mental institution. But her emergence from that institution and rebirth as an effective and innovative mental health worker is not simply a miracle. Her dedication to self-healing, her persistent attempts at creating a helpful environment, and her willingness to receive support from those around her, reveal her recovery as the outcome of careful and courageous self-examination and hard work. And Marie's unerring eye for the humor in her situation helped her fight against the spreading despair that came from being labeled hopeless. It was ordinary human efforts—extraordinary only in their dedication and persistence—that allowed Marie's faith to grow, bringing her spiritual sustenance, so that she could be healed beyond her own and others' expectations.

Marie's life story is deeply heard whenever it is told; it deserves to be heard more widely. It is a story of care and caring within a tangled web of neglect and abuse, of rebirth and inspiration amid the threatening atmosphere of chronic defeat. "We need to have hope for *every* person," Marie says. Her life story convinces us there is no other alternative.

I'm honored that she has asked me to collaborate with her in telling her story. My background makes such a collaboration exciting and rewarding. As a community psychologist, I've done research on the healing experience and community healing systems in different parts of the world for nearly twenty years. I've always tried to learn more about the process of healing, especially its origins in the individual and the community. As a clinical psychologist, I've also been dedicated to applying insights from healing systems in other cultures to the problems of mental and community disease in the United States. I've learned that health and healing come more from love and respect, for oneself and others, than from any specific therapeutic technique. The potential for self-healing and healing from within, both for individuals and communities, is a resource too often overlooked. Working with Marie is a rare privilege; her life offers and illuminates insights about healing and instructs us in the challenge of making these insights practical vehicles of change.

Marie's story is subtle and complex, not a tale of "good" versus "bad," nor "triumph" over "tragedy." It is a life unfolding, composed of ordinary experiences and situations punctuated, at times stimulated, by moments of insight and courage.

Marie was not a "mental patient"—even while she was in the hospital. Nor is she a "former" or "recovered" mental patient—even as she is lecturing to one of my psychology classes at Harvard. These labels hide rather than reveal the person. They dramatize to the point of caricature, distancing us from others so that we need not relate to them. Marie is a person whose life experiences, though different from most, have never robbed her of her humanity. At the very depth of her psychosis, she could touch her own wish for sanity even though this touch required every bit of her will to live. From the curled-up position of catatonic silence on her hospital bed, she could still see herself: "I looked at myself and said, 'No more. I can't go on this way anymore . . . if I ever want to get out of here, if I ever want to get better.'"

Now a highly respected professional in the field of mental health prevention and rehabilitation, Marie refuses to describe herself as "cured." She feels such a label ignores the process of getting and staying healthy. "When I was released from Sutton State Hospital, I didn't come out 'well.' It was a process of getting well. In my first years out, I would sometimes have to sit rigidly by the door, stuck in my anxiety, disconnected from my feelings. I still had to learn that I couldn't demand love and attention—I had to learn to exchange feelings."

Marie's working philosophy as a mental health professional is refreshingly simple. She emphasizes "client autonomy"—the development in clients of "inner controls." Her programs are characterized by an open, family approach which maximizes communication between staff and clients, minimizing bureaucratic obstacles. Her belief is firm: "Never write anyone off, no matter how hopeless they seem. You'll *want* to . . . but you never know. They took bets on me that I'd have to return to the hospital, but look . . . I made it!"

Today Marie is back at the state mental hospital in which she endured so many years of pain—but today she is Director of Community Affairs for that very hospital. People sometimes ask, "How could you return?" Marie sees no problem. "I accepted the position," she says, "to help bring high quality care to a place that was struggling to improve its services." It is more than optimism which guides her actions. Her most recent commitment, the Peacemakers, a spiritually-directed musical group now touring the country, demonstrates that. Marie's faith grows deeply, bringing hope to others whom she reaches.

Marie's life is a story worth telling and she is committed to telling it as a way of helping others. She speaks of working for "my people," the "hopeless, homeless people whom I understand because I know firsthand the depth of their rejection." But telling the story has a problem. Marie is concerned that she will be set up superficially as a role model. "I don't want clients to get the uncritical message that 'because I did it they can do it,' " she says, "and I don't measure clients' success by productivity or achievements but by the quality of their life."

Sometimes, after people read about Marie, they sense a similarity between her life and theirs or that of one of their friends or relatives, so they look for clues about what they or their family member should do in order to get better. Unfortunately, a few focus too much on what *Marie* felt and did, looking to her life as a model to imitate rather than as an example to guide or inspire them. Marie is not offering a recipe for recovery, with precise ingredients and stages. There are as many different stories of recovery as there are different persons living them. Her wish is that others may learn from her life what they can, taking only what they find useful, and living out only what is in their *own* life's path. That is why we have not analyzed Marie's life, trying to explain why she got sick, or how she managed to leave the hospital. As with all of us, Marie's life is dynamic, overflowing beyond set borders and categories, resisting neatly packaged explanations.

But it is what Marie's life *can* teach, and teach all of us, that has brought me even more closely to her. For I see in Marie's struggle and hope, in her way of healing, the process common to healers throughout the world. Marie's message speaks to our hearts, to the deep, spiritually deep wounds within, and from those depths offers the hope for a way out. And this is how real healers practice, emphasizing this kind of heart-talk and heart-work.

As I reflect on the many traditional healers I have worked with, in different parts of the world, I realize that Marie shares their perspective, and that Marie's process of healing is in harmony with theirs. Striving to remain honest, to remain real, when these traditional healers meet someone who needs help, they relate to her or to him as a *person* living in *community*; they don't treat the person as a "patient," or worse as a "sickness" which must be isolated from the community. They emphasize health, not disease; and they do not see disease merely as something to be conquered and removed from life, but respect it as an intrinsic part of the person and of life itself. These healers are servants of the people, sharing their knowledge and expertise rather than hoarding it. Most important, the spiritual dimension is the basis for all their healing work. The power of healing stems from a spiritual source and is given to the people. Through this exchange, healing becomes a renewable resource; the more healing is received, the more there is to give. As all participate in this process of giving and taking, healing continues to expand—more healing becomes continually available for all.

This spiritually-oriented approach, exemplified by traditional healers in less urbanized parts of the world, and practiced by real healers everywhere, contrasts sharply with the approach which now dominates Western biomedical health care. This Western approach, when it becomes too extreme, emphasizes care-givers as "experts" who "isolate" the problem and then "remove" or "conquer" it; they manipulate a "problem situation" or a "problem organ" rather than working with a person who needs help. An obsession to remove symptoms, to identify single causes, ignores the richly complex nature of disease and its multiple sources. Disease is no longer respected as one part of living. Nor is the spiritual dimension considered, either as part of the sickness, or as part of the healing. Because the number of such experts is by definition limited, and because the client and the community are cut off from rather than enlisted in the treatment effort, Western bio-medical health care remains scarce and costly.

Marie's struggle against the health-denying elements of the mental health system is a struggle against this skewed form of care. She refuses to be cut off from community. She fostered a healing community around her to assist her transition to health. The steps taken were often deceptively simple. After Marie moved out of the hospital, when she first visited her next-door neighbor for a cup of coffee, that was a very important experience. Here she was, drinking coffee with a regular person, a woman with a husband and kids, who lived an ordinary life in an ordinary apartment. It was all so normal—and powerful. Because now Marie, just by being there, normally being there and being normal, felt normal. Was . . . and is . . . normal.

Marie insists on her humanity, creating a respect for herself as a person whose history included mental illness, never denying that illness by exiling it to the taboo status of a "problem." Struggling against the dehumanizing anger thrust upon her by the abuses of her situation, she turns instead to forgiveness.

Marie left the hospital. In that sense, she has "made it." But when you meet Marie you know this is not a person who has stopped growing; she is trying, searching, walking toward boundaries. The fuel of her earlier struggle has been clarified, even refined, and now feeds her sense of mission. And like the work of true healers all over the world, this mission is based on a respect for the ultimate force of spiritual healing. In Marie's life, the power of spiritual healing worked and is working. Therefore Marie cannot claim personal credit for her recovering, nor can she pin down the exact reasons for its happening. What she did—and does—is to remain open to this spiritual healing power, both for its own sake and so that other treatments, including interventions based on Western bio-medical science, could be more effective. Marie prepares the soil.

Who can say when her illness began? Or what started it? Or what made her finally change? None of these questions can be answered simply—there is no single solution. In fact Marie's inching toward health continued, even while her behavior said otherwise. She acted toward health when she was able—and ready. The very fact that the spiritual dimension is beyond us—while within us—makes an essential part of the process of health and sickness beyond our understanding.

We cannot completely control our lives; we cannot determine precisely where and when and how we get sick, no less where and when and how we get better. But we must do our part—as Marie did . . . and does.

I'm reminded of what Toma Zho, one of the old !Kung-speaking Zhun/twa healers, tells me. In my book, *Boiling Energy*, I'm a messenger for his words, lived in the far reaches of the Kalahari Desert. "We try to heal people," he says. "We do whatever we can to help. But it is up to God whether we succeed or not." Marie and her story are part of this ancient lineage of healers and healing.

As Marie and I begin our collaboration on her story, we confront other problems. We have two autobiographical manuscripts to build on: one, written by Marie in the late 1970s, which she describes as a "rough draft," and the second, the product of a collaboration with a professional writer. These manuscripts describe the outline of her life events and associated feelings. But how can we fill out the total picture, so that Marie emerges as a real person—and is such a "total picture" even possible?

We spend many hours talking about her life. We feel that the "real" Marie can be found in the details of her experiences and as Marie speaks of these experiences, we bond together through our tears, as we share in abandoned laughter and the quiet of cutting pain. It's not easy for Marie—memory has safely stored some of those experiences as tales to be told, not lived. But our aim gives us the needed motivation—and we laugh more than we cry, which makes a big difference.

There are times when Marie is overwhelmed with the very emotions she felt more than twenty years ago. Often as she tells about a particular experience she's reliving that experience as we sit in my office. When the emotions are those of fear, anxiety, and terror, the new living is almost too painful. When the emotions are those of joy and excitement, the new living energizes Marie through deep laughter. And then there are the old experiences which are never fully described, too frightening still in their threat to become alive.

Working alone at home on a passage describing Marie's encounter with sickness or loss, I'm with her in her intense pain, her wordless fright. I don't want to go on, but am compelled to . . . and when the writing is over, I'm exhausted and relieved. I telephone Marie, ostensibly to give a progress report, but more wanting to talk. She's there, supportive: "Dick . . . I know what you're feeling. I'm sorry you have to experience those things." I'm glad she's there, and then I'm able to reassure her: "It's O.K., Marie . . . working with you on this book is my choice. I'm taking it on because we can all learn from those times of terror. And you're the one who *lived* the terror . . . I'm just helping you write about it." Marie's life radiates out, warming me, bringing me in.

As we share drafts of the book, it's wonderful to hear Marie say, "Yes, that's just how it was. I can't believe it . . . it's just like I'm talking with people back there in the hospital!" Those moments of recognition bring tears— sometimes of joy about a prank she played in the hospital, sometimes of sadness about a fellow patient who met a tragic death. And from those tears we know the book is working, and through it, Marie is speaking.

We also realize that Marie's life story is being created while we talk; in our exchange—both giving and receiving—Marie is not simply recreating feelings and reliving events; new meanings are found, new insights generated. Marie is living her life in the telling—her life story goes beyond a static repetition of past events. A life history, we learn, is but a particular form of a life being lived. We cease being obsessed with accuracy and seek truth instead.

Finally, we come to the question of "voice." Whose voice will speak in the book? Marie's? Which Marie? How is Marie's life to be presented? Whose material is it? From whom? For whom? We decide to follow the example of a person of wisdom who considered these issues. Black Elk, a Sioux medicine man, wrote the following to introduce his life history, *Black Elk Speaks*:

My friend, I am going to tell you the story of my life, as you wish; and if it were only the story of my life I think I would not tell it; for what is one man that he should make much of his winters, even when they bend him like a heavy snow? So many other men have lived and shall live that story, to be grass upon the hills.

It is the story of all life that is holy and is good to tell, and of us two-leggeds sharing in it with the four-leggeds and the wings of the air and all green things; for these are children of one mother and their father is one spirit.

Once we begin to understand Black Elk's words, we begin our collaboration in telling Marie's story. It will be, we hope, a story which is many stories, changing in the telling because it is alive. It will be, we hope, a story which is about Marie but not Marie's, because it is meant to serve others. It will be, we hope, a story for you who have come to this book.

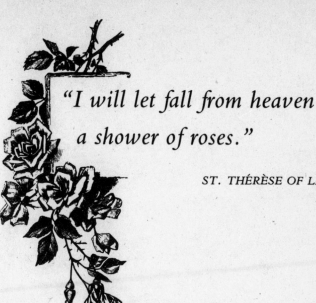

"I will let fall from heaven
a shower of roses."

ST. THÉRÈSE OF LISIEUX

NOBODY'S CHILD

1. *A Place of Terror*

*I*t's late afternoon and I'm sitting in the small kitchen off the open ward at Sutton State Hospital where I'm a mental patient. I'm talking with another patient while we smoke our cigarettes.

"How're you doing, Marie?" she asks me.

I hesitate. "Not too well," I respond.

The open ward has become a place of terror for me. Everywhere there seem to be spaces which are empty, and I fear falling into them, becoming lost and alone. I always retreat to a corner or a small place like the kitchen where I can feel the walls around me. I need protection.

Without my realizing it, the other patient has left the kitchen. My head begins to spin in a backward motion. My stomach feels icy. A surge of panic strikes me. I'm spinning and spinning. What's happening to me? I can't reason things out though I keep trying. Everything is spinning backward, racing out of control, and I know something awful is about to happen. I try to seize control but can't—it's a terrible moment. My whole mind, my whole body is going. I clutch my head to stop the spinning, but I feel myself going deeper backward in time, falling backward into a tiny space, unwinding backward, my skin becoming unraveled.

I grab my head again, pressing my temples at least to slow down the spinning. I keep trying to be myself, to be reasonable, to calm myself by saying, "This can't be happening . . . this isn't me," but it's useless. Terror overwhelms me. I feel ready to black out. I know I'm about to lose my mind and break down completely. I get very nauseous.

The spinning stops.

The intense panic, which has lasted several minutes, is over. I look down at my legs and arms; they look short, like a child's. I get up from the chair and start to walk towards the outdoors. I feel the size of a child. I'm a little girl of five. When I reach the front of the building, I can see the bright, colorful flower beds that have been recently planted. They should be beautiful to look at but as I gaze down on them, they look like rows of graves. I'm in a cemetery lot. My body feels heavy and I feel death take over. I sink to the ground and wait, thinking that I'm dying, but nothing happens. I remain lying on the soft green grass, completely enveloped by fear. I lie there alone, doing nothing.

"Marie, how are you? You O.K.?" one of the patients calls across the lawn. I get up and walk toward Dr. Baylor's office. I feel very small and it takes a long time to get there. As I walk, I begin to think of myself as Pat. I'm no longer Marie. I'm Pat. I've become who I once was—Pat, the little girl of five before she was adopted by Ma and Pa and had her name changed to Marie.

"Marie, how are you today?" Dr. Baylor is cheerful in her question.

I stand there, shifting from foot to foot, feeling embarrassed.

"Is there anything I can do for you, Marie?" The doctor's voice is a little more concerned, as I slump and curl inward, hiding my face from her.

"Marie . . . Marie . . . are you all right?" she asks, now more earnestly.

I reach for a pen on her desk and scribble on a piece of paper: "I'm not Marie. I'm Pat."

More than twenty years ago in a mental hospital I struggled through that terrifying regression into my childhood. As a woman, Marie, already in her mid-thirties, I became Pat, the child I once was at five years old. And I suffered through many other experiences both in and out of the mental hospital. Now, however, as I look back on my life, I can honestly say I wouldn't change it. The pain and suffering have brought me psychological understanding and spiritual strength. I still feel the pain when I reflect on those experiences, but while once they would throw me deeper and deeper into anxious despair, now they feed my desire to keep growing.

My earliest recollections of myself are of that little five-year-old Pat, and of how I was forced to make the abrupt and confusing transition to become Marie when I was adopted. It's there that I can begin my story.

2. *Ma and Pa*

*M*y life really begins in Gloucester, Massachusetts, when I was five years old. Ma and Pa have just adopted me and changed my name to Marie. One hot summer day shortly after I've come to live with Ma and Pa, I hear the shrill, sing-song shouts of the neighbor's children: "We know who you are . . . we know who you are! You don't have a mother! You're adopted." Angry and frustrated, I run to Ruth, a friend of Ma's. Tears fill my eyes and stream down, wetting my cheeks.

"Why are you crying?" Ruth asks.

"The kids . . . the kids say I'm adopted," the words barely escape through my sobs.

As she gently wipes my face, Ruth asks me what I think "adopted" means.

All I can say is, "I don't know but it's awful bad!"

Age five, I feel unloved. I feel that I belong to no one and deserve the hatred and contempt of others.

Born in Boston, Massachusetts, in 1930 during the depression years, I am the child of an unmarried alcoholic mother. She names me Pat. I have no knowledge of my father and live with my mother for only five years. Things are difficult. When I'm only a few weeks old, in the bitter cold of January, she has to walk through the streets of Boston, holding me tightly in her arms to keep me warm, as she goes from door to door begging for milk.

My mother has two other little daughters, one older than I and one younger. I don't know why my sisters remain with her while I don't. When I'm five, she places me in a foster home run by the Valentis.

Not long after, a woman comes to visit at the Valentis' home. I can't understand the relationship between this woman who speaks strange words and Mrs. Valenti. Later I learn that the strange words they speak are called Italian. The woman, Mrs. Bartello, comes to visit several times with her niece, Sarah. Then one day I'm told that Mrs. Bartello will be my mother! Shortly after that I leave with her and move to Gloucester.

The Bartello home is a two-family structure sitting directly on a beach that seems to stretch for miles. Between the garden and the water's edge is a long brick wall which breaks the rising waves during the height of a storm. It seems like a foreign land and I'm overwhelmed with confusion. The confusion also comes from another change: the Bartellos have renamed me Marie. What did I do wrong as the young child Pat to make them drop that name? I can't figure it out.

The transition to the Bartello home in Gloucester is difficult. Mr. Bartello is fifty years old and Mrs. Bartello, five years older. They're too old to adopt a child of five. Neither of them speaks English and I have no knowledge of Italian.

Soon after my arrival, Mr. Bartello sets down three rules, and demands their strict obedience. The first rule is actually easy to follow—there will be no mention of my life prior to coming to Gloucester. I think the Bartellos are very nervous about adopting me and want to insure that I'll accept only them as my parents. And that's what happens. I accept Mr. and Mrs. Bartello as my mother and father from the very start. They are the only people I ever address as my parents. I know them as "Ma" and "Pa."

The second rule shuts me down cruelly—anything that occurs within the Bartello home is not to be discussed with anyone except Mr. and Mrs. Bartello. That prohibits me from speaking up when I'm most unhappy and fearful. The third rule cuts most deeply—no tears are to be shed in the presence of Mr. Bartello. There are so many times when I feel on the edge, pushing away throbbing tears in order to please Pa—pushing back my feelings into a deeply unavailable space. I'm terrified of breaking the rules and suffer from fearful compliance—my emotional life begins to starve.

My adoption becomes the "big secret" within the entire family. I realize that I must never mention the adoption to the Bartellos. It's as though it's something bad that should be hidden. I don't know what the word "adopted" means but as I learn from other kids' cruel teasing, I come to my own understanding—being adopted is not just being "different" but "bad." I keep this secret sense of my own badness locked within me until I'm fourteen—the first time I really let on to anyone that I know I'm adopted.

Ma is very austere. She always stands erect and wears her hair high on her head, pulled loosely back in a pug. She is Victorian in her thinking; her attitude toward men and sex is that they are not to be mentioned by nice young ladies. She has never conceived and knows little about raising children. Ma doesn't show her feelings to me.

When I try to be close to her she pushes me aside. I want to snuggle up onto Ma's lap, where it will be comfortable and warm. Instead, I have to restrain myself so that I won't offend her. I wonder why it's right for other children to be cuddled but wrong for me. Her only means of showing affection is to shower me with lots of toys and pretty clothes.

For years I have a feeling inside which I can't understand. It comes when I feel close to someone. I think the feeling is something dirty and bad, and it isn't until years later that I discover the feeling is love.

Though Ma and Pa try to make me happy, my life with them is very lonely. Pa was a widower before his marriage to Ma. From his prior marriage he has a son, Marco, who has been living in Italy. Now that Ma and Pa have adopted me, they think it would be good to send for Marco so that the family will be complete. Marco arrives during the year that I come to Glouchester. He is twenty-two. My loneliness continues to grow, especially after Marco's arrival— he is a brother but not for me, as the age gap between us proves too great.

There are other relatives within the family but I'm estranged from them the moment I come to Gloucester. Ma has several nieces who feel very close to her, but resent my becoming a Bartello, jealous that I may some day inherit a portion of the Bartello estate. I'm too young to understand the source of their resentment and spend many confused hours brooding over their hatred of me. It's especially hard for me because it seems they get along so well with Ma. I always wonder—"Why can't I be in this family, too?" I never think too long about the answer—it's too painful.

Instead, through reading, I begin developing my own private answers to my feelings of loneliness and rejection.

I take the characters in my children's books into my heart. They are my family. I begin to retreat into a fairy tale world where all ends well and the "charming prince" takes his newfound princess away to the "happy land."

The language barrier which exists between my parents and me doesn't last long. Within a year I'm speaking Italian fluently, and finally get accustomed to my new name.

The Catholic Church is very strong in our Italian-American neighborhood. Ma and Pa are Catholics, but there the similarity between them ends. Ma is part of a group of older women who go to 6:30 Mass every morning—regardless of the weather. They put on their black shawls and go—every day! That's just something they do. And every night I see Ma sitting by the stove, saying her prayers before she goes to bed.

Ma enrolls me in Sunday School, sends me to Mass on Sundays, and always stresses the Ten Commandments. Like most kids growing up, I don't want to be "preached to" about religion. Yet there develops in me, even at that early time, a spiritual strength, and I think it emerges from the atmosphere created by Ma and those old women.

Pa is a different story. He believes very strongly that Christ is merely a man, not the Son of God; a great prophet, an extremely giving man, but not Divine. He talks about the value of Judaism even though he's a baptized Catholic. Pa is angry at the Church. He grew up in Italy and lost his parents when he was very young. As was common then he was raised by his godparent who was also a priest. One day his godfather heard him swear and made him—though he was only nine—go around the entire church and lap the floor with his tongue. His tongue and mouth became infected and swelled into an agonizingly grotesque expression. After that, Pa turned fiercely against the church and ran away to sea as a cabin boy. There he was exposed to a variety of religious ideas from the people he met from all over the world, confirming his anti-Catholic position.

Pa always tries to influence me toward his ideas. We'd be sitting at the table and he'd say, "Oh no, Christ is not the Son of God," or "the Catholic Church is just trying to get our money," or "that priest is up to no good." I'm afraid of Pa so I just listen, never disagreeing with him even though I say to myself, "He's wrong. I know he's wrong." At night, alone in bed before I go to sleep, I pray, and sing myself to sleep with devotional songs. My father doesn't know I'm singing religious music because he hasn't been inside a church and doesn't recognize those songs. I sing the songs in English and since he speaks only Italian, he doesn't realize the content of my songs.

There I am, a child of nine, deeply—and secretly—involved in a devotional life. My prayers help overcome some of the intense loneliness I feel—through prayer I have someone who cares for me. But because of Pa's anti-Church attitudes, I enroll in public rather than parochial school, an unusual decision in our intensely Catholic neighborhood. It's not until I'm a teenager that I attend parochial school because Ma feels a teenager needs the discipline of a Church environment. Pa reluctantly agrees.

Pa's a commercial sea captain who owns his own fishing vessel. A vigorous man who works hard and takes pride in his vessel, his greatest fault is his violent temper. His stubborn and domineering personality pervades the entire Bartello household. He's used to commanding a ship and runs his home the same way.

For many years, I live in mortal fear of Pa. He's a strong man and rigid disciplinarian. To me, as a young child, he's overwhelming. I obey him without question. He never strikes me—he never has to. He always speaks to me in commands, with a stern, unyielding voice. That's enough.

Whenever I'm disobedient, he sends me into the cellar until I've learned my lesson. The cellar is a dark, bleak place where Pa keeps his fishing nets and boat equipment. Standing in the center of that cellar, with the nets shedding ominous shadows against the gray walls, I'm terrified. A sick feeling covers me and settles in the middle of my belly. My head feels like a revolving ball of thread that will swiftly unwind itself. I move quietly toward the head of the stairs. Slowly I creep to the top landing where I can see a ray of light shining through a crack in the door. The sight of the light calms me and I wait. Ma and Pa know I've sneaked to the head of the stairs. I can see them sitting at the table laughing at me for trying to fool them. Eventually they let me in and I go to bed—shaken and relieved.

At home I feel mostly fear, never knowing when I'm going to do something wrong, always knowing something I'll do will be wrong—and then Pa's violent anger will be aroused and I'll be locked in the basement or a closet, an "evil" child punished for her "sins." What I do wrong always seems so minor compared to what I know goes on with the other kids in the neighborhood—maybe not keeping my room clean or coming home a little later than expected—but for Pa and Ma these are "transgressions," really "bad" behavior, and the punishment must be severe. And whenever I do something "wrong," Pa hits Ma. I'm petrified when I hear him screaming at me and Ma, and I pray to Our Lady, strongly but under my breath, that he won't hit me. Pa's so unpredictable. I never know when he'll come home from his fishing trips, and whether he'll be happy or furious when he arrives. I have premonitions about his coming home, and they fill me with a sickening dread.

Once I get outside, things are different. We live in a fishing community—almost all the men work out at sea. Our Italian-American neighborhood is close-knit, and there are more than twenty of us kids playing together in all different kinds of groups on the small street. This is during the War years, so being of Italian origin isn't so good. The prejudice of outsiders toward our neighborhood—we are called "fascists" and "Mussolini lovers"—bonds us together.

I really enjoy the special occasions we have during the summer months. We kids go out to the rocks along the ocean shore beneath a tavern where wealthy tourists come, and dive for pennies they throw into the water. We divers are a tight little group, and we go for the coins more for the fun of it, and to show our strength, than for the money. Then there are the nights when the mothers gather together in the street, build a bonfire and play around, acting foolishly, dancing with abandon. It's wonderful to see older women having so much fun. The men, they just sit quietly on the benches by the beach, talking about fishing.

We kids have our own special times together. Every Sunday we go to a matinee movie—*if* we do our homework and housework on Saturday, including washing down the front stone stairway, and attend Mass on Sunday. Every Saturday afternoon we go to confession, and we begin to gossip when one of us stays too long in the confessional!

I like being outside, being part of the gang. But I'm outside so little. Ma restricts me to the house. She's afraid I'll get in with the wrong crowd. I feel cut off, always looking at the world through my window. My home imprisons me.

It isn't always bad between Pa and me. I also have pleasant memories of him that I'll always cherish. There are the evenings when Pa is home from fishing and we sit together at the kitchen table. He tells me the stories from operas such as *La Boheme* and *La Traviata*. Many evenings we sit by the old phonograph and listen to the great Italian singers such as Enrico Caruso, and Pa extolls their beautiful, powerful voices.

There are other good times while living with Ma and Pa, especially the Christmas Eves at cousin Lena's. Cousin Lena is a wonderfully happy and generous woman with a large extended family. They celebrate Christmas Eve together, and my last Christmas Eve with them I remember best. I'm thirteen. Ma and Pa never go to Cousin Lena's to celebrate Christmas Eve, preferring to remain at home alone, but they allow me to go because they understand that I want to be with the other children.

Even before entering Lena's house, I'm in a festive mood. We begin our celebration with the traditional feast which lasts until midnight. All kinds of fish are displayed on a long table—baked stuffed shrimp, fried smelt, octopus, and even baked stuffed quahogs on a half shell.

At midnight the young people attend Mass and when we return Lena is frying Italian sausages and making fried dough—the strong, delicious smells permeate the entire house. After everyone has eaten, the table is cleared and we play poker for pennies. Everyone is included. The game goes on until early in the morning, accompanied by constant jokes and much laughter.

Shortly after coming to the United States, my brother Marco marries Ma's niece, Sarah, and again I'm an only child. Ma and Pa keep me isolated from many neighborhood activities. Ma had waited a year before enrolling me in school, saying I need time to adjust to my new surroundings. I feel different from the other kids, cut off from their easy laughter.

When I begin school I do very well academically but have a difficult time getting along with other children. The kids who live in my neighborhood know about my adoption and the word spreads throughout the school. Not knowing how to react, I become very argumentative and often feel rage rising within me. This further alienates me from the group and my loneliness increases. Literature again becomes a true friend. I'm reading all the time, which drives me further apart from other kids. I'm very fond of Dickens. I admire his stories, like *David Copperfield,* in which a child overcomes great odds with persistence and courage. And here I am, not overcoming anything! Ma and Pa are happy to see me reading a lot and have great expectations for my future. They dream of my going to college and becoming a doctor or lawyer.

Adolescence brings new problems. Ma is terribly strict and keeps me close to home. My contact with boys is almost nonexistent. At first, I don't understand why boys have become bad people and why I should fear them. Later, as I learn about sex and babies, I become very careful about the way I dress and act around boys. Many of Ma's fears rub off on me and I've become quite inhibited. For example, because Ma feels there would be too many boys there, I never attend a football game until long after high school graduation.

During my adolescence I begin to wonder who I am and where I came from. I know I had a mother and often, lying in bed at night, I wonder what she was really like. I like to think of her as a kind woman who was warm and gentle. Why I assume she's dead I don't know. Perhaps that's the only safe reason I can find for her having abandoned me. Yet I continue to daydream that she's alive and will still come back to me. Once, when Ma ties me up in the cellar for being rude to her, I ask God to send my real mother back to me. Since Pa isn't home then I don't have to fight back the tears.

Though my adolescence with Ma and Pa is filled with emotional conflict, it's brief.

I'm fourteen and a freshman at St. Agnes High School. Pa's rigid rule is that I have to be in the house by the time the street lights are on. One evening after visiting with a new neighbor, as I walk back toward my house, I'm gripped by a painful tightness in my chest. The street lights have just been turned on! By the time I reach the house, I can see Pa in the window—he's furious. I'm almost too scared to go any further, but it's a cold night, and the darkness makes me want to be inside. I go up to the door. "Let me in . . . please, let me in." I'm so afraid I can't even speak these words—they stick in my throat. "I'll be good, just let me come home." I'm choking on my own words. I want to cry but seeing Pa stops me short—never cry in front of Pa! His face is impassive, etched in fury. Abruptly, and without any change in his emotion, he pulls down the shade. It's as if a boulder has just hit me on the head; I feel like I'm going to collapse. The sound of the ocean has become eerie. I'm so frightened I don't know which way to turn. I pound on the door, let me in . . . let me in—but the house is still. I'm lost, so very lost. Without thinking, I go back to the neighbor's house, anxious and confused. They let me spend the night in one of their spare bedrooms but sleep won't come. All night I worry about what the next morning will bring.

When morning finally comes I leave the neighbor's home and go to St. Agnes's Convent to see my friend, Sister Paula, but she convinces me to return home. There I'm confronted by a Miss Whitcomb, a social worker whom I've never met before. She seems to have taken over the house. Ma and Pa sit quietly in the background.

"Is there anything you can tell me about your side of the story?" Miss Whitcomb's question surprises me.

"Does she really want to know what happened last night?" I wonder.

She persists, "Tell me anything you want to about what's been going on. I'm here to help you."

I feel Miss Whitcomb is my ally and that gives me strength. But another person seems to be talking when I begin to speak—the Marie I know never had the courage to go against Ma and Pa's wishes in front of others. I don't tell about all the hurt, sadness, and fear I feel being with Ma and Pa—that's too much. But I do speak about my unhappiness, my wish to be somewhere else.

"I don't want to stay in this place . . . I don't want to be here." My words are as painful to me as they are to Ma and Pa, who sit there, just listening. I can see the hurt in their eyes.

"And I don't even belong here. I'm adopted." I blurt out. Another rule broken. Ma starts to cry. Now I've crossed the line. It's all over. I've betrayed them. Ma and Pa look so defenseless, so beaten down. Sure they tried. They gave me all the material things a young girl could want. I feel ashamed that I'm so ungrateful. Yet something in me holds on, and I insist again, "I want to leave this place." How many times have I wished to leave, dreamed of a better place waiting for me? "This is my chance to go," I think to myself, and again I speak words which seem to cut into Ma and Pa, "I want to go . . . now!"

"It seems clear to me," Miss Whitcomb intones, "that it would be better for Marie to be placed elsewhere. I hope you'll agree." Overcome by the situation, Ma and Pa's continued silence is their assent.

"There's this nice boarding school in Boston that would be happy to take Marie. I think she'll do well there," Miss Whitcomb continues.

"Boston . . . but Boston, it's too far," Pa interjects. Miss Whitcomb goes on at some length about the virtues of the school. "It will be best for Marie," she asserts. Pa reluctantly consents.

One week later, accompanied by Ma and a neighbor, I board the train to Boston, carrying everything I was going to need in one small suitcase.

3. St. Therese's Home

*I*t's late August and the day is sunny and warm. A cool breeze blows gently across my face and it feels good. It's only a ten minute walk to the Gloucester Station, but Ma and her friend walk so slowly it seems we'll never get there. It's an hour's train ride from Gloucester to Boston where my new residence—St. Therese's Home for Girls—is located. I'm really looking forward to a new environment. I wonder what St. Therese's will be like and if the Sisters who run it will be kind. Maybe the place will be gloomy and I won't like it. From the train we take a street car. I'm still anticipating St. Therese's when we stop. I can't believe what I see.

On the side of the road are beautiful homes that look like estates of the wealthy. Carefully manicured lawns encircle each house and huge, tall elms line the street. Across the road is a large graceful pond. It reminds me of a picture postcard. Can one of these houses be the "Home"? When the conductor shouts, "St. Therese's!" I'm overjoyed. Right now life seems really good to me.

St. Therese's is just as beautiful inside as it appears from the outside. Ma and her friend speak to each other quietly in Italian, "This is a nice place. They'll take good care of Marie here." Since neither speaks English I act as an interpreter and make all the introductions. I feel shy and somewhat apprehensive in the presence of the Sister who greets us. I hear the voices of girls from another part of the house and wonder if I'll "fit in." Ma and her friend are served tea by the Sister who informs us that she's in charge of the girls and will see to my needs. She also explains a little bit of the daily routine and tries to allay any doubts Ma may have. Ma and her friend don't remain too long. As Ma is leaving, I feel only guilt. Perhaps I'm being selfish for not considering her wish to have me home.

The first staff person I come to know at St. Therese's is the Sister Superior, Sister Clara. She's so cheerful. We all want to be with her; her infectious smile and enthusiasm make us feel good. All the girls respect her; she's dedicated to her work and involved with each of us personally. Sister Clara's a disciplinarian, but for me in a new way—she's firm but also fair. I don't fear her and can only marvel at—and be grateful for—the difference between her and Pa. Most important, I discover Sister Clara sincerely loves all the girls—and I come to love her too. My memories of her are with me even today, strong, clear, and nourishing.

Fifteen girls are living at the Home, most either orphaned or from broken homes. We are all of high school age and upon graduation are not allowed to remain. I make close friends with two of the girls almost immediately and get along very well with most of the others. A sense of camaraderie exists among us, and we enjoy the usual boarding school pranks, like throwing someone in the shower fully clothed. At night, Sister Clara goes from room to room wishing us a goodnight and dousing us with Holy Water as we lie under the covers giggling.

Our daily routine is very relaxed. We begin with a mandatory Mass at 6:30 A.M. After breakfast each girl makes her bed, straightens out her room, and completes a chore such as cleaning a bathroom or helping prepare meals. The worst part of preparing meals is peeling potatoes. No matter how much we clean them Sister always finds a spot we missed. I often wonder why potatoes are such an important part of our diet!

In good weather, we spend our leisure time outside, playing croquet or badminton. There are picnic tables set up where we can have our lunch. The grounds are spacious with secluded spots where we can sit quietly. During bad weather we spend our time in a recreation room on the top floor, listening to music on the phonograph, sitting around, sewing, talking. During the school months, the recreation room is used as a study hall where, after supper, we all sit quietly, doing our homework. All of our time is spent either at the Home or at school— we are allowed to go into town only when absolutely necessary. Though the rules are strict, I'm happy at St. Therese's.

At St. Therese's I attend St. Mary's Academy, a private girls' school whose students come primarily from middle class Catholic families. I really enjoy St. Mary's, and make friends with Sister Nicky, my English teacher. Sister Nicky is a tiny woman in her early thirties with a big heart and a warm smile. Pa gave me a love of literature; Sister Nicky helps my interest blossom. Under her influence I begin reading the works of Shakespeare, Shelley, and Emily Dickinson. Sister becomes my confidante, and our friendship continues after I leave the Academy. Five years after my departure, I lose contact with Sister Nicky—I miss her terribly, for she was my best friend.

But I don't do well academically at the Academy, and the Sisters at St. Therese's are disappointed, especially Sister Clara. She feels that I have special abilities and don't work up to my potential. Though I enjoy St. Therese's I do miss Ma and Pa. I also miss my few friends back in Gloucester. Yet, I don't want to return to Gloucester—all I think of is how unhappy I'd been there. Sister Clara gives me permission to work part-time at Presbyterian Hospital as a nurse's aide and my work there, together with school, keeps me busy, giving me less time to brood. My first job! Trying to fulfill its requirements shows me how immature I really am.

At the end of my junior year at the Academy, Pa requests that I come home to visit. Things go smoothly, but the old fears are still there and I know they always will be. When I'm preparing to return to St. Therese's, Pa speaks to me, "We wish you were home again. Won't you come back and live here again?" I'm still afraid of Pa and his question has the force of an order. But I know my mind. Still it takes all my courage to say no. I see Pa standing beside me with his head bowed. He's crying— and trying not to. I don't know what to do. He seems weak—I don't know him that way. Then I feel compassion for him, and sorrow. I'm tempted to change my mind. My feelings are very strong and I don't know why I don't alter my decision. But I return to St. Therese's after only two weeks at home.

A few weeks later, Sister Clara informs me that Pa won't pay my board any longer. She suggests that I return home. I'm stunned! I didn't realize how badly Pa wanted me home. I thought both Ma and Pa were resigned to the fact that I wouldn't return. During my two years at St. Therese's I've visited Gloucester only a few times, and Ma has visited me only three times. Wasn't that in itself enough to let them know how I felt about returning? Just before I felt good about my future but now that school has ended, I'm hurt and disappointed. I go to Sister Clara, and we cry in each other's arms. Even then, still sobbing, I keep insisting, "I won't go back to Gloucester. I can't go back there." With Sister's help I secure a full-time position at the Presbyterian Hospital and arrange to live in the nurses' quarters.

My job at the Presbyterian Hospital doesn't go well and I don't stay too long. I enjoy the work and the nurses are helpful but I'm frequently depressed, and those episodes, which last longer and longer, interfere with my work. I'm absent for days at a time and many times, while at work, I have to leave because I can't do the work assigned to me. All I want to do is lie in bed and sleep. I lose weight and suffer from persistent colds. I feel very sorry for myself; it seems that nobody cares what I do and that I have no roots. At seventeen I feel totally unprepared for the task of supporting myself. The supervisor at the hospital finally suggests that I leave the job and see a social worker at the public welfare agency in Boston. I relent.

When I meet Mrs. Lancaster, the social worker at the agency, I have no job, no money, and lots of self-pity. I expect her to perform miracles and give me instant happiness, but her simple kindness proves enough. Mrs. Lancaster arranges for me to live at the Weston Street Home, a residence for indigent women. Most of the women there are mothers with babies who are waiting for apartments. The Weston Street Home is an unpleasant brick building located in one of the poorest neighborhoods of Boston. It has very large rooms with faded grey walls and brown metal stairs with iron banisters. Meals are served in a large cafeteria with long wooden tables and chairs. The food is sparse and my teeth begin to ache from its poor nutritional quality. The only furniture in the rooms is cots set up in rows. All through the night I can hear the babies crying.

At Weston Street, I meet Ginny, an eighteen year old with long blond hair and blue eyes. Ginny always has a smile on her face even when things are going badly for her. We become friends.

One afternoon, Ginny and I go for a walk in the park. The summer sun feels good as we walk along, chattering nonstop. We're both disillusioned with Weston Street, and it doesn't take much talking for us to decide to leave the Home and take a trip to New York. At that time it was unheard of that teenagers, especially girls, would hitchhike, particularly out of state. Ginny and I are implusive when we decide to go—all common sense is outweighed by the excitement such a trip promises.

At six P.M. we get a ride with a truck driver who agrees to take us as far as he's going—New York. We travel all night, singing songs at the top of our voices. My depression leaves; I feel free and happy. Putting my past behind me, I don't give one thought to what I'll do when we reach New York. I just don't care.

By morning, tired and hungry, we have passed the outskirts of New York and, unknowingly, bypassed the city as well. The truck lets us off and we start to walk along the highway. We come to a dirt road and follow it for about a mile. When it ends, we are left speechless. We gaze across a valley filled with every shade of green imaginable, all blended beautifully. The grass is a velvet plane and the mountains lie serenely around us. It's the most beautiful spot I have ever seen. God must surely exist I think, for only He could create a world so magnificent.

We stand awhile in awe of the view before heading back to the highway. A car stops and two state troopers get out. We become very confused and have difficulty answering their questions. But they're friendly enough and take us back to the police barracks and feed us. We calm down, so that when the trooper arrests us for hitchhiking and vagrancy and takes us to the local police station, we aren't even upset.

The police station is relatively small with three spotless cells. Ginny and I are placed in the same cell so that we won't be frightened. We sing songs until early morning, stopping only for refreshments or to tell each other jokes. I'm not worried about anything. We're living just for the moment, making the most of a bad situation.

Later that day we're released and given train tickets to Boston. The train ride is uneventful, but I feel the old depression coming back again. The elation of the previous two days has left me and I feel confused by my past actions. I'm also worried about what I'll do when I get to Boston.

I go back to the Weston Street Home, but during the week my depression becomes more severe. My head feels as if a tight band is wrapped around it, and my body is so leaden that it becomes difficult to move. I spend most of my time lying on my bed either daydreaming or crying. How useless everything is. I no longer feel a part of the life around me and the more isolated I feel the more I isolate myself. My appetite's gone and I have no interest in anything, not even in reading which has always been a pleasant way of escaping my sadness. There's nothing more for me to do. In despair, I try to take my life, setting my clothes on fire. But as the flames start to grow, I become locked in terror, and frantically put them out before they touch my skin. I don't have the energy to do *anything*!

Mrs. Lancaster is alarmed at my condition. In her office I mention the fire I set to my clothes. I just want to cry, I'm so unhappy—but I'm also so tired and deadened, that I can't even feel my face as my own, and tears are in some distant place.

"Marie, tell me what's wrong," she asks, her eyes searching for an answer.

I remain silent, drooped into the chair.

"Marie, I think you'll have to go to the hospital . . . you're sick and need help."

Mrs. Lancaster's words come to me, but they're empty and they make no sense. I can't imagine what a hospital can do for someone like me since I'm not physically sick. But Mrs. Lancaster is so insistent that I decide to follow her to the hospital a block away.

4. *The Castle*

As soon as Mrs. Lancaster and I arrive at the Loring General Hospital, a young nurse in a neat white uniform ushers us into the admission room. In a professional manner she takes my temperature and blood pressure. I glance about the small room, with its examination table, grey metal supply cabinet and hospital-smell antiseptics. Over the loud speaker a doctor is being paged.

A few minutes later a tall, impressive looking man steps into the room.

"I'm Dr. Coburn," he says, as if to the room, overlooking me. His voice seems cold, his presence detached. He asks Mrs. Lancaster to leave.

"Now, tell me why you're here in the hospital?"

I can't answer . . . I don't know why and I don't have the energy to figure out why.

"Can you tell me what brought you here?" Dr. Coburn's questions are demanding. I feel trapped. His dark eyes are so serious they go deep into me and I'm compelled to avoid his glance.

"You must know why you're here," he insists.

Suddenly I realize I can't speak. Overwhelmed by all that's happening, I think no words can explain my deep sadness and depression.

I know only that there's no satisfaction in my life, and that the world is a cold place where I'm being forcibly detained. I want to hide away from all that exists. Seeking relief from my feelings of despair, I wish only to sleep and forget that I'm alive.

Dr. Coburn continues to press me for answers, but I remain silent. Finding his efforts fruitless, he leaves the room. The nurse helps me undress and put on a johnny. Before I realize what's happening, Mrs. Lancaster is saying good-bye and I'm being pushed in a wheelchair to the elevator, then up to the sixth floor to the psychiatric ward.

The psychiatric ward is small with only three beds. Later I learn it's an emergency care center for short-term patients who are transferred to other facilities within ten days. When we reach the ward a nurse takes my arm and helps me onto a bed in the center of a room. The room is completely bare except for a window with a heavy screen that prevents me from looking out.

My bed is in full view of the nurses' station and I can see them busy at their desk. Climbing into bed, I reach for the covers and pull them over my head. The darkness feels good. I'm safe, hidden away from the world. Hopefully nobody will take me away from my warm, soft resting place.

As I lie under the covers, the voices of the nurses are reassuring. Though I don't want to talk to them, I'm glad they're there. They'll take care of me. It's good to have someone else carry my life's burden. I'm secure . . . and totally dependent.

I remain in the psychiatric ward at the Loring General Hospital for three days. During that time I do nothing to help myself. I keep thinking only that I belong here and sink deeper and deeper into my bed, believing that there is nothing I have to do but exist, because others will feed me and tend to my needs. I speak only in monosyllables and refuse to eat. I'm trying to starve myself to death but the nurses and doctors persist in their efforts to get me to eat. They try to spoon feed me, coaxing me as a mother would her young child. I'm finally threatened with tube feedings, which really frightens me, but still I refuse to eat.

On the morning of the fourth day, an ambulance stretcher is shoved into my room and without any preparation, I'm told that I'm leaving the Loring General for another hospital. I'm scared . . . no one is there to help me. People are just milling around or passing me by, and when they tell me to go somewhere or do something, they push me. Although I can't understand why I'm going somewhere else, I don't ask any questions. Inside the ambulance I'm numb from anxiety and confusion. A nurse from Loring General rides with me in the rear of the ambulance but gives no comfort. Within thirty minutes, the siren is still and we're at the Merrimac State Hospital.

I've never been in a psychiatric hospital like Merrimac before. I'd heard of people going to the "nut house" but had no idea that such places really existed. And to think I could be in such a place! When I realize where in fact I am, I become so frightened I feel myself shaking violently, though I remain rigidly still. Mired in a stupor, I want to run out the door, but can't move. The ambulance driver and nurse from Loring leave me in the admission room. I'm a wounded animal weakly struggling against the painful iron of an unexplained trap.

A nurse helps me undress, giving me a johnny to put on. As she takes my temperature and blood pressure, a young doctor enters the room. He speaks in an unintelligible accent. Several times the nurse has to help me understand his questions. I'm terrified and try desperately to still my tears. There is a hard lump in my throat and my lips quiver uncontrollably.

The doctor writes something down on a sheet of paper, says something to the nurse and leaves. The nurse tells me the doctor will give me a physical later.

"I'll need your clothes," she says as she takes them off me. "The shoes and socks you can keep wearing. Your clothes will be sent to the ward." As she speaks she wraps me into a multi-colored bathrobe—at least two sizes too large.

In that bag of a bathrobe, I'm taken to West One. We pass through the door and enter into a big day hall. It's almost empty of furniture except for a few wooden benches along the dark green walls. A ping-pong table is set up in the center of the room and black iron bars line the outside of the windows. The air is musty and the combined stench of urine and disinfectant repels me, making me feel dirty. Patients are standing around idly; their hospital robes hang on them in disarray, here and there exposing sections of their decaying nakednesss

I'm not prepared for what I've just experienced. To me, hospitals are places where you go when you're physically sick and leave when you're well. The nurses wear white starched uniforms, with little white caps on their heads. They move about an equally clean and white environment, caring for the sick with gentle kindness. But I'm not sure any kind of preparation would have been helpful. I'm barely seventeen and terrified.

We walk into a small room that serves as an office. A young nurse sits at the desk and looks up as we approach. She's introduced to me as Mrs. Corcoran.

"This is Ward One. I'm the head nurse here. Let me know if you need anything." Mrs. Corcoran pauses briefly, and looking at me for what seems too long a time, asks, "Do you need anything?"

I remain petrified. If I respond at all to her words, I can't tell. I'm in a daze, buffeted from the outside by frightening sights, and from the inside by anxiety. I'm afraid to look at anything or touch anything.

"You can go back into the day hall, if you like. Dinner'll be in a few minutes," the head nurse continues.

As if released from my stupor, I leave the room and walk into the day hall. There I meet up again with fear. A disheveled woman about forty years old approaches me. Her hair is stringy and unkempt—it looks like it hasn't been combed for days. She has pancake make-up plastered all over her face and bright red lipstick is smeared outside the edges of her mouth. Her clothes, many sizes too big, with their oddly matched colors, make her look like a scarecrow. She stops in front of me, balancing jerkily on her bare dirty feet. She looks grotesque.

I slowly move away from her. I don't want to speak to her. I don't even want to see her.

"I'm Lady Esther. I'm sure you know that!" The woman's voice catches me as she steps into my path. "I can help you, I can make you better, you don't have to be crazy, to be crazy, you don't have to be, I can be your doctor." Lady Esther rambles on and on, shifting chaotically from foot to foot.

"This woman is crazy!" I think. "She's crazy . . . and so is every other patient in this room except me." My thoughts race, "I'm not like these people. I don't belong here . . . I don't belong here."

I start to scream at Lady Esther to get away from me and out of nowhere, several nurses rush to my side.

I begin to sob loudly and my words pour out incoherently, jagged and sad, "I'm not crazy . . . I'm not really crazy . . . can't you see that, don't you see me? I'm not like those ladies. Take me out, I don't belong here!"

The nurses hold me, tightly but softly. "You're all right . . . we know you're just fine . . . you'll be just fine," one nurse says as she guides me over to a bench. She remains with me for a while, calming me down. I become quiet. Her presence is comforting, and my fears slowly go away.

It doesn't take long to become somewhat adjusted to the surroundings. After the noon meal, student nurses arrive in their gingham uniforms and white starched aprons. They're refreshing after the dismal morning and soon I'm talking to them, enjoying the attention I'm getting. We play ping pong and toss around a ball. I ignore the other patients, thinking I'll also be considered crazy if I associate with them. I want to be different, to protect myself from being called "crazy." It's easy for me to be different since I'm the only teenager on the ward and, compared to the others, able to carry on a normal conversation.

In the five short days I remain at Merrimac I become very comfortable. I get used to eating my meals with a large spoon, since forks and knives are not allowed. I get used to the irrational and bizarre behavior of the other patients and manage to get enough sleep even though my bed is inches away from the babbling voices of others. There are some night nurses who are mean-spirited, speaking to us in harsh, demeaning language, abusing some of the patients physically as well. But other nurses treat me with understanding and that seems to make up for all the negativity on West One. Soon I'm wishing I can stay on the ward. It's a home for me. When the staff tell me I'm being transferred to a hospital closer to my area of residence,

I cry. I'm certain that whatever contentment I've found at Merrimac has ended and that I'll never find such understanding again.

My tears are useless. The very next day I'm sitting in an official state car, on my way to another mental hospital, Sutton State.

As the car approaches the town of Sutton, a huge building, sitting high on a hill, comes into view. It's massive and majestic, but forbidding. It looks like a rambling medieval castle with its tall steeples stretching upward into the sky. My stomach feels queasy and as we near the grounds an uncontrollable fear takes hold of me. The car moves slowly up a winding road. Beautiful tall elms line each side of the road and I smell the freshly cut grass. The car stops and the nurse who accompanies me from Merrimac steps out. She leads me to the entrance of the building marked "Admissions." What I soon learn to call the "outside world" is left behind me as I anxiously, and with great hesitation, enter Sutton State Hospital—called by patients and staff "the Castle." The year is 1948. I'm seventeen.

In the admission room, the staff take all my clothing, even my pocketbook and ring. An attendant in a grubby white uniform with shoes run down at the heels comes into the room. Unpacking my suitcase, she jams all my clothes into a bundle to be sent to the marking room. All I can do is wonder how I'll get the wrinkles out of my blouse and slacks when I get them back.

"You can't have your shoes back for a couple of days," she says without looking at me.

I can't believe my shoes will be gone, but I don't have the energy to object, and barely have the energy to put on the pair of cloth scuffies she gives me. I tie the scuffies around my ankles, but they're too big and I know they'll fall off. The nightgown the attendant gives me is several sizes too large and the bathrobe reaches down to my ankles. I feel like a dwarf in giant's clothing. The admission process has stripped me of everything I can call my own. It's taken my sense of self right away from me.

A doctor arrives. He sits at a table next to my bed and begins writing on a sheet of paper.

"Do you hear voices?" he asks in a flat, distant tone.

I can't imagine what he's talking about, and my expression remains blank.

"What month is it?" The doctor's question seems so odd and cold. Does he really think I can't answer such a simple question correctly? But again, I'm so surprised, I say nothing.

"What year is it?" he continues.

"Maybe I really am crazy if he asks me those kinds of questions." I think, but all I can do is sit and say nothing. I'm frozen with fear and confusion.

Finally, the doctor seems to lose interest in me and he routinely takes my blood pressure and listens to my heart and lungs. Without a pause, he proceeds to give me a brief sermon on the virtues of good behavior. I listen but give no response, not even a nod of my head.

"Take her to B-1." His words are an order to the attendant. I want to ask the doctor, "What's B-1? What'll happen to me there? Where am I going?" But before I can form the questions, he's gone.

The attendant puts me in a wheelchair and pushes me down through many long corridors, each containing row after row of neatly made beds. At the end of each corridor, a heavy brown metal door closes noisily behind us. As each door closes, I feel the "outside world" fading further . . . and further away. I'm lost.

B-1, I later learn, is where all new admissions come although the ward is almost totally filled with elderly patients. All I see are old women shuffling around in confusion. The youngest seems about seventy. They're milling around, some of them in nightgowns and some of them naked. I'm so stunned by what I see that I become numb and my mind goes blank.

The attendant takes me into a room with a huge white tub. "All new patients have to have a bath and shampoo when they first come into the hospital." The attendant's words are not reassuring.

As she starts the water running into the tub, she tells me to get ready. I don't know what to do. Finally I feel compelled to remove my nightgown, and as I stand by the tub, I try to hide my nakedness with my arms. Embarrassed, I climb into the tub and begin to bathe. I allow the attendant to wash my hair—that feels good. But as I sit in the huge tub, the voices of the old ladies resound in my ears and fear fills the hollow of my stomach.

After completing my bath, I have to answer more questions for my admission record. Then the attendant tells me to go to the sunporch. "Could I have a cigarette?" I ask meekly, even though I really need a cigarette since I'm a smoker.

"Smoking only after meals and with supervision," the attendant responds as she leads me to an alcove in the center of the long ward and through a pair of double doors into the sunporch. The sunporch has huge windows covering one entire wall. There are no curtains, and except for several wooden benches and straight chairs, the room is completely bare. As I enter, I'm confronted by about fifty old ladies wandering around going nowhere. I have to be careful of stepping into puddles of urine on the tiled floor.

An obnoxious stench of urine and feces fills the entire room. My terror couldn't have been any more if I had been hit by a truck. The old ladies are moaning and crying. Some of them are strapped into the straight chairs with sheets tied around their waists. Their nakedness shocks me. I go to one of the many windows and weep. Looking out at the smooth, well-groomed hospital lawn, I'm utterly desolate inside. "This is the end of my life," I think. "I'll never see the outside world again." And as a picture of Ma and Pa Bartello forms in my mind, I ask myself, "How . . . just how have I come to this end?" I can only weep more for my answer.

Dinner's at noon and it's mass confusion. The meal is served on metal trays; the only utensils, large spoons. The old women patients sit on wooden chairs and many of them have spilled more food on themselves than they put in their mouths. Abused by the constant shouting of the nurses, they are crying pitifully. I drink a little milk and walk back into the ward. I wait for smoking time to be announced. After an hour, I'm led into the bathroom where three other patients join us. They ignore me. We're each given one cigarette. I try to make mine last as long as possible, smoking it until I can't hold it between my fingers any longer.

"Remember that one . . . the next cigarette won't be until after supper," the attendant barks. I wonder how I'll manage to wait so long.

After smoking time is over, a big tough nurse with red hair approaches me.

"You have to return to the sunporch now!" Her words leave no room for discussion, but still I wonder why the other four younger patients, who are also on the ward with me, don't have to go to the sunporch. My instincts take over, and I tell the nurse I won't go.

"You'll go . . . and if you don't, you'll be sent to A-2."

I don't know about A-2 but sense it must be pretty bad if the nurse is threatening me with it. Yet, I can't budge from my resolve.

"You go to hell," I blurt out, and immediately panic as I imagine the consequences of those words, regretting they ever came out.

The red-headed nurse gives me a frightening look and walks away. For about a half hour I sit shivering, expecting the worst. I feel sick to my stomach and want to vomit.

Without any warning, a group of nurses comes charging through the door of the ward. They're coming toward me! I'm terrified. Two of them grab my arms and push me out the door; the others follow closely behind. My screams and tears are futile as they drag me up the stairs. Before I know it I enter what must be Hell and I just want to die!

Ward A-2 is dismal looking. With its poor lighting and dull yellow walls, it's like a dark cellar that's been raised to an upper floor. There is a long row of beds against the wall, each with a yellow bedspread pulled tightly across it. Otherwise the room is bare, with the exception of a small table at the end serving as a desk. The stench of disinfectant and urine stifles me, and the shouts of attendants drown out the cries and moans of the disturbed patients. In an effort to get a shine on the floor, two patients are pushing a polisher by its long wooden handle. To the right of the ward is an open doorway to the sunporch, which is now blocked with a wooden bench. Through the door I see women in institutional dresses that fit like large sacks with an opening at the neck. As I look around, I feel sick in my stomach—such a place seems inconceivable. What's happening to me? I can't understand it. But here I am, in the back ward of Sutton State.

The attendants deposit me in the sunporch. Their keys hang loosely from chains wrapped around their waists. I feel as though I'm in a prison. Some of the patients are walking in a circle around the sunporch. Their loud screams hurt my ears. They're all ages and many are naked. Conversation with most of them is impossible, for they're mentally deteriorated. I sit in a corner, trying in vain to ease my intense fright. I see no hope of escaping from my situation and feel it's useless even to suggest that I want to return to B-1. That's what really disturbs me.

The afternoon hours go by. I remain in the sunporch until 2:30 P.M. when a new crew of attendants comes on duty and removes the bench from the sunporch doorway, allowing us to leave.

Mealtimes provide the only diversion, especially since I'm allowed to help with the evening meal. I set up the tables, serve food, and then wash the trays and spoons. The attendants are pleased that I'm helping, and I soon learn that doing such work is the only way to get in their good graces. Because I've helped, I'm allowed to smoke. Again smoking is restricted to the bathroom. As several of us smokers stand in a corner of the bathroom, patients come in and out to use the facility. All toilets are visible with only a partition between them for privacy. A couple of patients pee on the floor right in front of us. An attendant comes toward them, shouting furiously at them to get a mop and clean up the mess. We carry on our own business, smoking our lone cigarettes, trying to remain cut off from the pitiful plight of those women splashing their own urine about with their uncoordinated mopping.

In spite of the terrible condition of A-2, I become absorbed by that back ward environment and the shock of being there subsides. I still want to leave A-2 and ask often to be returned to B-1, but in the two days I'm on the back ward I've begun to adapt.

Now as I look back on that time, I'm amazed and saddened. I needed so much to feel accepted and taken care of that I sought and found some comfort even in the midst of the oppressive environment of the back ward.

The evenings on A-2 are more pleasant than the daytime hours. Most patients climb wearily into bed at five P.M. and sleep soundly until it's time to arise at four-thirty A.M. The evening crew are friendlier and have more time to talk to those of us who can communicate. It's during those quiet evening hours that I also become aware of the seclusion rooms. I hear the pounding on the seclusion room doors and the garbled shouting of those who cannot safely be let out on the ward or who are sent to seclusion as punishment. It would have been easy to observe the patients in seclusion rooms through the small window on each seclusion door, but I stay away, afraid I'll see more than I can stand.

At 9:30 in the evenings I climb into the bed assigned to me. The beds in the ward are less than a foot apart, and I'm engulfed by the disrupted sleep of others. The rubber mattress is stiff and musty. Even the pillow is unyielding, for it's made of straw. At 10 P.M., when the night crew arrives, the first sounds I hear are the slamming of the door and the jingle of keys. Those sounds haunt me for a long time— I never get used to them. As I try to sleep, the cries from the seclusion rooms punctuate the quiet, darkened ward. The night nurses set themselves up in comfortable chairs at the end of the ward, and wrap themselves in sheets so they can sleep. It's dark except for a few dimmers near the door.

On my second evening in A-2, at 2:30 in the morning, I have to go to the bathroom. The bright bathroom light that's kept on all night blinds my eyes momentarily. A couple of patients are huddled in a corner sneaking a cigarette. They have evidently stolen matches, which is strictly forbidden. I join them for a smoke. My heart is pounding. I know I'm breaking a rule and can be severely punished. As we stand there smoking, a figure appears out of nowhere and fills the doorway. We're caught! Guilt and fear come at once. I'm glued to the floor. Another nurse comes in and they grab me roughly by the arms, drag me to a seclusion room, and shove me in. The door slams. I'm completely alone with only a rubber mattress on the floor, an indestructible blanket, and my nakedness. My nightgown has been ripped off and taken away.

I throw myself down on the mattress, cover myself, and begin to sob uncontrollably. As the darkness of the room engulfs me, I ask God to please take me. I beg Him, telling Him I'm not afraid to die. I wait, but nothing happens. When I realize that death is not coming, I just lie there and gradually my tears subside. I remain awake the rest of the night. At 6:30 the door opens and I'm let out—shaken and confused.

Breakfast soon arrives and I put the horror of the night behind me. I hope that this day I can return to B-1. Much to my surprise, I'm taken there that afternoon. I'm glad to be back, sensing my freedom there.

There are abusers in the back wards and the front wards too. But there are also those in the front wards who are sympathetic to me. When I come back to B-1 it doesn't take long to learn who the "good" nurses are. As soon as I return, I walk up to one of the attendants and offer to help with supper. I expect to be sent to the sunporch, but instead, the attendant asks me to sort the laundry in the clothing room. I readily agree. I learn that the afternoon shift is short of help and welcomes my work. I sort all the laundry, help feed the elderly patients, and clean the kitchen. I even wash the kitchen floor with a mop that seems to weigh more than I do! As a reward for my help, I'm given a hot cup of coffee and an extra cigarette. Several nurses are very friendly and willingly listen to my life story. I tell them about living with Ma and Pa in Gloucester and how I came to the Castle. Later that night I go to bed feeling good about the attention I got. It was worth all the hard work.

The following day goes in the same fashion, and I discover that work is really the solution to the hated sunporch. I'm never kept there again. The head nurse on B-1 insists that the younger patients be productive; otherwise, out to the sunporch they go! I remain in her good graces for the rest of my stay there.

On my fifth day in Sutton State Hospital I meet Dr. Pearl. She tells me that I'll be going to the staff conference the next morning. At the conference the hospital doctors determine whether to commit or discharge the patients who are admitted, as I've been, on a "pink paper" for a ten day observation period.

"Marie, you might be discharged tomorrow." Dr. Pearl's words are kind, but they make me very anxious. "I really don't think you're sick enough to be here at the Castle," she continues. "You belong back home, outside. Do you want to go back to your home with the Bartellos in Gloucester?"

Ma and Pa had not been notified of my admission to Sutton State since I'm now eighteen and no longer a minor. Dr. Pearl's description of their house and Gloucester as my "home" seems strangely distant and frightening.

"I don't want to go back to Gloucester," I reply without hesitation. "I think I should go back to Mrs. Lancaster in Boston. She'll find me a place to live."

I'm glad when Dr. Pearl agrees to my plan, but the real truth is that I don't want to leave the Castle. I know in my heart that Dr. Pearl is right. I'm not sick enough to be in the Castle. I'm not like those other patients, but still something in the Castle is drawing me in. Though I've spent only five days on B-1, I've already come to value the security and personal attention I experience there. I'm not a free agent at the Castle and the surroundings are depressing, but I'm willing to give up my freedom to stay there.

I miss being able to have a snack whenever I want, and sleeping late in the morning. I also miss the privacy of a bath and being able to use a toilet without someone watching over me. I particularly miss the luxury of a toilet with a seat. Yet I would choose to remain in the Castle.

That night I don't sleep well. I'm anxious about leaving and worried about my future. I also worry about the staff conference. Morning comes too quickly and at eight o'clock I'm sitting in an anteroom next to the hospital's main conference room. The thought of going in and being questioned scares me, and I feel nauseous. Within a few minutes Dr. Pearl comes out, greets me, and leads me into the conference.

The room is filled with people—doctors, supervisors, social workers, psychologists, head nurses, and student nurses. I keep my head down as Dr. Pearl ushers me to a chair that is placed in full view of all. I quickly sit down. One of the other doctors introduces me to the group and starts to interview me. I want to hide, to crawl away from the crowd of people who are watching me, waiting for my words. The doctor's questions are so personal, yet I don't even know him, and most of the other people in the room are unfamiliar. I can barely respond as question after question comes toward me, asking about my thoughts and feelings, what I do on the ward, where I want to go after leaving the Castle.

"Do you want to die?" The doctor's question hits me unexpectedly. I'm deeply embarrassed. My words become hardly audible, and I can't be sure he can hear my soft "no."

I'm like a laboratory animal being dissected before a large audience, like an insect ready to be crushed by people in white coats. My emotions are overwhelming and when the doctor begins to ask me about my life growing up in Gloucester, my eyes fill with tears. I bite my lower lip very hard so as not to burst out crying, creating a worse scene. I'm aware of all the people sitting attentively in front of me and can feel their eyes staring at me. When they finally tell me I can go, I get up from the seat and walk steadily out of the room. Later that morning they tell me that I'm discharged.

At one o'clock I say good-bye to my new-found friends in the Castle. I try to be cheerful, but I sense even then that it isn't a final good-bye.

5. *"This is Your Mother"*

*I*t's fall 1948 and I'm an immature eighteen year old returning to the outside world with great hesitation, even anxiety. Being small in build, about 5 foot 2 inches and a little over one hundred pounds, my physical appearance remains that of a young girl, mirroring my state of emotional development. Yet as I sit by the open window of the bus which takes me from Sutton State to Boston, my mood lifts. The gold and red leaves of the elms brighten the sky, and the cool air, with its clean smell, gives me energy. I tell myself that I'm more fortunate than those I've left behind at the Castle, but still I regret leaving that place. I know there won't be anything better waiting for me in Boston. I have only five dollars that one of the nurses generously gave me and a suitcase full of worn-out clothing. My mood has lifted but my future looks bleak and already I long to go back. For now, however, going back is impossible.

It is mid-afternoon when I arrive in Boston. It's strange being in the city with hundreds of people pushing and shoving. They all seem to be going somewhere so important that their lives depend on how soon they get there. I go directly to the Welfare Agency to see Mrs. Lancaster. She's said to be expecting me but I dread seeing her again. I haven't seen her since that day she left me at the Loring General. I'm ashamed that I had then to be placed in the Castle, a state psychiatric hospital.

I walk toward the Welfare Agency offices and everything looks the same. I smell the familiar stale odor of the old building—it reminds me of an old schoolhouse on the first day of classes. Mrs. Lancaster gives me a big smile and welcomes me like a long lost friend. My body relaxes and the scared feeling ebbs away. We talk for a long while. Before I leave, she arranges for me to live in a room in downtown Boston, providing me with enough money for room, rent, and food.

My "new home" in Boston is but a room in a three-story walk-up and though it looks pleasant enough, it feels like a place in which I'm condemned to suffer a slow deadening of my feelings. Almost by the hour, the furnishings become colder and harder, forcing me out to the street. The wallpaper, decorated with a floral pattern, seems shabbier and shabbier, the occasional smudges and stains standing out more and more, overcoming the gaiety of the brightly colored flowers. The bed, which at first seems soft and receiving, increasingly begins to smother me, as I sink into it so deeply it's hard to get up. And I don't want to get up . . . but I feel driven out of the room.

Out in the street, things are not better. The car horns amid the heavy traffic create a noise that hurts my ears. Surrounded by people and clamor, I'm lonely and wish that I were someplace else. Hundreds of people pass me by; they are close enough to touch but miles away. I trudge along the street with my head bowed and my shoulders hunched over. My blue jeans and sweatshirt add to my "lost soul" look. I'm in no mood to take the trouble to dress up.

Eating provides no relief. My appetite is almost nonexistent, and I don't want to go to public eating places because I feel so uncomfortable around strangers. I end up several times a day in one little diner close by my room, mostly drinking coffee, picking at food I order, staring into my plate, crumbling up my napkin. The waitress fortunately leaves me alone—otherwise I think I'll have to flee, but since I'm so weak and tired, I'll probably just burst into tears.

I've been in Boston only four days but I already know the end of my stay in the city is near. I go back to the Welfare Agency. Mrs. Lancaster beckons me into her office. By the way I look it's clear that I'm very depressed. "I just feel awful, all the time," I blurt out. "All the time I'm alone, and unhappy. It's like I'm a stone that just keeps rolling downhill."

What I'm trying to express is that I'm going downhill fast and can't stop myself from going into a deep depression. Mrs. Lancaster understands that and is alarmed. Because of my past depression, she's concerned that I might again be thinking of taking my life. She urges me to return to the hospital, and I reluctantly agree. I'm really ambivalent. I want to be where it's safe, but yet, I hesitate to give up my freedom entirely. As soon as I agree, Mrs. Lancaster arranges for me to return to Merrimac State Hospital. By noon I'm on a stretcher in an ambulance and on my way.

Though I've gone through the process of entering state psychiatric hospitals in the past, I can't stop the queasiness building up in my stomach and the incessant pounding in my chest. The ambulance drivers push my stretcher into the admission room. The same supervisor who admitted me less than two weeks ago is there. I know that she hadn't expected me to return so soon, and I feel guilty about being there again. The supervisor has little to say and hurries me into the now familiar johnny and bathrobe and directs me back to West One.

As we near the door of West One I smell again the disinfectant and urine. Now I fully realize where I am and begin dropping into a state of utter discouragement. But still I'm relieved to be back in a familiar place—relieved even though I feel awful about being caught up again, and so rapidly, in the oppressive dreariness of the ward.

Mrs. Corcoran, the head nurse, welcomes me back pleasantly and assigns an attendant to get me something to eat. The meal is over so that only cold cereal and toast are available. I'm not very hungry so I eat only a slice of toast and drink a cup of milk. Then I go into the day hall and sit in a corner. I look around for Lady Esther but she isn't there. I can't recognize any of the patients and later learn that the patients I had known have all been transferred to other wards. West One has become a receiving ward for new admissions.

On my second day at Merrimac State several student nurses try to speak to me in the day hall, but I refuse to talk to them. I'm very discouraged now and want time to digest all that has happened to me during the past weeks. I also want time by myself to get used to being back in the hospital. Since I've been here, it's like a dream—I still don't believe it's happening to *me*. I sit in the corner all afternoon.

At 7:30 that night, the nurse in charge comes over. "Marie, you've got company. They're waiting for you. You can see them in the doctor's office."

"Who's there?" I ask with some hesitation. I don't want visitors.

"Your cousins from Gloucester. They want to see you," the nurse says enthusiastically.

I'm surprised and feel uneasy. I haven't seen any members of my family for several months. "What are they doing here?" I think, and then I wonder, "Are they here in this hospital?"

"I don't want to see them," I state after a moment of indecision.

"But Marie, you should see them," the nurse counters. "They've come a long way . . . and they really want to see you." For several minutes she pleads with me, trying to overcome my opposition. "You shouldn't disappoint them. It'll be good. They like you and it's your family." I waiver, and reluctantly, I agree.

The nurse leads me out of the ward and toward the doctor's office. Butterflies crowd into my stomach—the nervous tension is building. I'm very ashamed that my family should see me in a state mental hospital. I go into the doctor's office where I'm left alone to wait.

I stand behind the doctor's desk facing the door, and in a few minutes my cousins Ann and Rory enter. There are two other women with them, but I pay no attention to them since they aren't familiar. Overwhelmed by this unexpected visit, I keep my eyes lowered. I nod my head slightly as they greet me and then there's a long silence. I'm very uncomfortable and wonder what the awkward silence means. Then Ann speaks up, saying to someone, "You tell her!" Again there is silence. Someone else blurts out, "You tell her!" I'm confused—I can't understand what I'm supposed to be told and why they're reluctant to tell me. I look up at the group.

Still silence. An agonizing tension engulfs the room. I'm bewildered, and just as I'm about to ask, "What is it?" I hear the words, "Marie, this is your mother!"

My head starts to spin and I have to hold onto the desk so I won't fall. I feel shaky and then numb all over, and for a moment the room fades away. Then, slowly, I feel myself returning to reality and I try desperately to regain my composure. Everyone is waiting for me to speak, but the words won't come. Then, tears fill my eyes and I begin sobbing. As I cover my eyes with my hands, words of comfort reach my ears. I feel close to my cousins for the first time—and at that moment we are sharing something very special. They begin to talk but all the while I'm in a different world, not quite real.

After my tears subside, I lift my head, searching for a glimpse of the woman who's been brought before me as my mother—a tall, thin woman of about forty with soft blue eyes and long brown hair that falls loosely just above her shoulders. I want to feel her warmth and love—I've waited so long for her to come. But at that moment, all I feel is my own longing for love. It's difficult for me to know what she's like or what she's feeling because, though she's my mother, she's no more than a shadow that I'm attempting to reach in any way I can. She's no more than a stranger in whom I'm placing all my hope for happiness. I want to say so much to her but can say nothing. Neither of us speaks. I want her to know how often I pray for her to come and fill the emptiness in my life. I want her to know how much I need her and how lonely I've been most of my life. Instead, I say nothing.

Standing behind the desk, stunned by what is happening, I'm further surprised as my cousin Ann introduces my older sister, Gerry. Gerry, like mother, is tall and thin. She has long, auburn hair and blue eyes that match beautifully with her light complexion. Ann also tells me I have another younger sister, Renny. "It's amazing," I think, "a family of my own . . . and after all these years, it's happened so quickly!"

It's a very happy time for us all, but too brief, as the supervisor comes to take me back to the ward. As the group starts out the door I call my mother to my side, telling her I want to speak to her alone. Neither she nor my sister has said much tonight and I want to talk to her and feel her close to me. I'm afraid to let her go because I don't want to lose her again.

Mother and I stand facing one another and in the instant our eyes meet, I feel like a little girl. Such mixed feelings are churning through my head, and my heart pounds as I nervously try to find words to tell her how long I've waited for this moment and that somehow I've always known she was alive. This isn't an easy moment for her either—she too is groping for words. She makes a strong effort to ease the tension and suddenly we're embracing. It's just a brief, somewhat awkward moment but I feel totally comfortable in her arms. She promises to return in the morning to take me home with her. Then she's gone.

Back in the ward, I just go to bed. I want to be alone. I don't feel like talking about the night until I've sorted things out in my own mind. The nurses understand and leave me alone. I'm unable to grasp fully the meaning of the night's meeting, but after an hour of tossing restlessly in my bed, I finally drift into sleep. The next morning after breakfast mother and my two sisters come for me. I'm truly happy for the first time in many years.

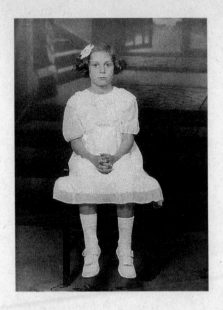

Marie at first communion

Ma
Pa

Sutton State Hospital
(courtesy Salem Evening News)

Tunnel to cafeteria in Sutton State Hospital
(© 1991 by Dorothy Littell)

Marie and Marlo Thomas, who played Marie in the TV film about her life

Marie at work

Joe

6. *Back Home to the Castle*

As we drive toward their home in the town of
Lenox, I still can't believe I'm with my newfound family.
I'm on edge—excited and happy. Mother explains to me
how she's found me after these many years. She had agreed
to sign the adoption papers on the condition that she be
given the name and address of my adoptive parents, Ma
and Pa Bartello. I think of how unusual that condition is.
Why would Ma and Pa allow that? Mother had decided
that when I was eighteen she would find me. And she's
true to her word—I'm just past eighteen! She went to the
Bartello home looking for me. Pa had just received a letter
from Merrimac State reporting that I was a patient there,
so that very evening arrangements were made for mother
and my two cousins to see me. As mother is speaking,
questions come to mind that I want to ask but I sense that
it's best not to. Who and where is my father? Why did
mother keep my two sisters with her and place me for
adoption?

These questions would never be answered.

My sister Gerry talks excitedly, trying to acquaint me with the various members of the family. She tells me we'll be seeing my maternal grandmother who lives with them. My younger sister, Renny, is also with us in the car. I marvel at her shiny dark eyes and long wavy black hair. Her features are much like my own and she's petite like me. I've never known what it's like to share family resemblances— I'm really glad I look like my sister.

As we drive into a poor neighborhood, we stop at a large run-down tenement house. It isn't like Ma and Pa's home, which is fairly new and well cared for. I'm dismayed at the condition of the tenement, but the idea of being with my mother and my two sisters keeps me in a happy, excited mood. I'm home now where I belong and that's all that matters.

We climb the stairs to the second floor and walk into an apartment that's neat and clean. Despite its lack of modern conveniences and cheaply made well-worn furnishings, it's warm and comfortable. It feels like a real home. Secretly I hope that this place will be my final stop. Already I've told my mother that I want to finish my last year of high school here in Lenox and perhaps go on to college. She seems pleased.

As soon as we enter the apartment, my grandmother rushes to greet me, hugging me warmly and generously. She's a big woman with short grey hair. She, like my mother, calls me "Pat." My new family calls me by the name given me at birth. It's confusing to be called Pat after all these years as Marie, but I want to go along with the wishes of my new family.

Mother seems happy to have me home and I feel loved and wanted by her. I think of living in that house as a normal person with a regular family. The next day, I register as a senior at Lenox High School and begin classes. But I'm very shy in the classroom and feel terribly awkward. To make matters worse I'm placed in the wrong division—I want college-prep courses but end up in the business section. Though disappointed I say nothing to my mother when I return home that day—I don't want to risk upsetting the good feelings at home.

The first three days at home are full of contentment, though I remain on edge, not wanting to upset things. On the fourth day things change radically. I attend classes as usual and get home about 4:30. When I enter the apartment, my mother is sitting in a chair, disheveled and pale. My sister Gerry is standing beside her, and when I walk over to them, Gerry turns her face away.

"What's going on? Is something wrong? Is mother sick?" I keep questioning Gerry because I can't understand what's happening.

Gerry keeps evading me but finally mumbles, "Mother took some pills with her wine."

At first I don't comprehend, but after the shock of my mother's appearance wears off, I put things together and realize that my mother is an alcoholic. It feels like the floor has just collapsed under me! As I stand by my mother's side, she says nothing. I want to run away as fast as I can but I can't move. Then, abruptly, mother gets up from her chair, puts on her coat, and walks unsteadily toward the door. I go out after her, Gerry's words ringing in my ears.

I follow my mother down the stairs and into the street. Somehow I sense that she's going to a bar, and as we walk along, I become more and more depressed.

"Mom, let's go home. Let's go home now," I plead, tugging at her arm. She starts walking away from me, and I hold onto her even more tightly, pulling her toward me.

"Take your hands off! Who do you think you are?" she says angrily, turning toward me. "You go home. Just mind your own business and go home."

I'm in the middle of a nightmare. Is my mother really saying this? Is this my mother?

"Please, please come back," I implore, standing in the middle of the sidewalk, crying and begging her to come home.

She walks on, as if I don't exist, then goes into a cheap cafe. I look inside but she's gone, part of the crowd at the bar. Feeling helpless, I turn away and start walking. For about an hour I walk and walk, up and down the streets, trying to understand the situation. But the more I think about it, the more confused I become. What a dirty trick life has played on me. I don't want to return home, so without really thinking, I go back to the Castle. It seems like the Castle is all that life holds for me. I go to the station in time to catch the 7:20 bus.

It's a bitter cold night with a sharp west wind blowing as the bus drives up the familiar winding road toward the Castle and I'm scared. Will I be admitted? What will the staff's reaction be when I ask to be taken in? I'm depressed and angry at the same time and all I want is a place to hide and forget the past week, particularly tonight's events. I hurry to get into the Castle building where it's warm and go directly to the admission office. I'm shaking and weak.

"I need help . . . I need help now," is all I can say to the supervisor on duty. The admission process doesn't take long. Predictably, I'm being pushed in a wheelchair through the long corridors, the sound of heavy metal doors slamming loudly behind me now offering a strange reassurance.

I can hear the familiar whining of the old ladies lying restlessly in their beds. It's after ten o'clock and the ward is dark except for the dimmers. After my shower and shampoo I'm assigned a bed close to the nurses' station and as I lie there quietly, I think of how I'm going to blank out everything that has just happened and not discuss it with anyone at the Castle. "I'll just wipe it out of my mind," I sob to myself as I fall into a fitful sleep.

I remain at the Castle this time for about a year. I spend most of my time on C-1 which is an intermediate ward. Patients come to C-1 from B-1, which is for more disturbed people, and go from C-1 on to an open ward where they have the freedom of walking around the grounds.

The head nurse on C-1, Miss Harris, is a kind and gentle young woman in her mid-twenties. She always gives the impression of complete competence. It doesn't take long for me to feel close to her. I'm already disillusioned with two mothers and eager to trust someone like her. It doesn't matter that she's no more than five or six years older— she's still like a mother for me. Miss Harris spends a great deal of time with me and at one point gives me a picture of herself taken at her graduation from nurse's training. On it she writes, "To Marie. Remember, anything worth wanting is worth fighting for!" Those words mean a lot to me—and even more later in my life.

Life on C-1 doesn't seem so depressing because I feel there is nothing but heartache in the outside world. The Castle has more to offer. I have all the security I need and along with that there are all these potential mothers—the kind nurses—to love me. There are also about six adolescent girls on C-1 and we band together. We treat each other much like sisters and share cigarettes and money earned mopping floors. Although we're not allowed to smoke on C-1, Miss Harris often takes me down to the tunnel beneath the ward where, amidst bundles of dirty laundry, we share a cigarette and talk on and on like old friends. Miss Harris works Monday through Friday, and C-1 becomes two places for me, as the warm pleasures of her companionship during the week give way to a harsh loneliness on the weekends.

It's strange how Sutton has become my home—comfortable and comforting. I can never forget that we are locked in—there is the cold, hollow clanging of the keys which hang from the chain belts strapped around the nurses' waists and the penetrating slam of the metal doors shutting around me. But if we obey the rules we're taken care of—and that's enough because we can hardly expect to be really cared for.

Some of the rules deal with our beds. The wards have rows of beds, so close together we can't walk between them. The thin yellow bedspreads have to be tightly folded underneath the mattress, without a wrinkle left. The stiff pillow has to be puffed up to its full extension. During the day, the bed is not for our bodies. From 5 A.M. to 7 P.M. no sitting or lying on beds is permitted; from 7 P.M. to 5 A.M. we have to lie on the bed and sleep. These periods of forced sleep are at times a relief, at times a punishment.

The beds also become our storage areas. Since we have no bureaus or closets, we store all our possessions under the mattresses. Like all the other patients, I've become a hoarder, storing under my mattress what for us are precious items, such as food, toilet paper, sanitary napkins, magazines, and money. We don't always make the usual distinctions between the values of those items. In the closed environment of the ward, money isn't always the hardest thing to get.

Commands dictate our actions. The day begins with "Rise, ladies, rise!" and proceeds through the meals, "Supper, ladies, supper," until it ends with "Lights out, ladies, to sleep." If I follow the commands, perform chores, such as helping to bathe and feed the elderly patients, and obey the rules, I receive my three meals, I'm warm at night while sleeping, and I'm left alone, maybe even talked to.

But there's one experience that I never get used to. Three times a day I'm forced to eat my meals in a cafeteria that also feeds the patients from the back wards. "Cafeteria" is an overglorification. That place is no more than a filthy, gloomy tunnel where tables and benches are set up for male patients to eat in one section, females in another. Each day, three times a day, I have to stand in a long line waiting to get my food, while around me some of the pitifully dirty patients from the back wards are screaming obscenities, their limbs jerking wildly; others are moaning deeply inside their blank selves; others are merely shuffling along, pushed forward by those behind them. One of them always starts shrieking or gets into an argument or physically attacks another patient, and then large male attendants race over to subdue them, knocking those of us who might be in the way roughly to the floor or against the wall. And there's always some poor woman urinating or defecating right where she stands in the line.

Sometimes a sympathetic supervisor lets me cut ahead of that line, but most often, the attendants yell, "Get back in line! Who do you think you are? You're no better than anyone else here. In line lady!" I have to eat—and so I endure the line. And eat what? I hate the food, and the time spent in line waiting for it makes the food even more disgusting. I never feel satisfied, though I'm not hungry. We can't go back for seconds, so many of us fill our trays with six or seven cups or coffee, preferring that drink to the watery, tasteless food.

Yet, even with this daytime nightmare of the tunnel, or should I say "cafeteria," Sutton State can be comfortable and comforting. My needs are great yet it doesn't take much to satisfy them. And there are the good times—especially with my friends. Our group of adolescents hangs out together. We try to make sense of our rapidly changing bodies and emerging emotions, the way other teenagers do, except that we're in the mental hospital rather than the shopping mall or high school parking lot. It isn't easy though, as each of us has problems, and when they become severe, it's often more than the group can deal with. At such times we become cut off from one another as we retreat into private fears and anxieties. But there are also times when we rescue one another. By calling everyone together for a group activity or exploit, we can pull one another out of a personal maelstrom. There is a solidarity among us. We feel like we're all in the same boat, that it's a stinking world, but "What the heck, let's forget it for a while."

We enjoy breaking the rules of the hospital. That's what they're for! How else can we keep our spirits up and have some fun in what has to be one of the world's dreariest places? We're still young, and though we suffer the anguish of our mental disturbances, *we* know that we're different from those old women who shuffle achingly along the hallways and remain listlessly drooped in their chairs. They're the "back warders," the pitiful ones; we're still human—and feeling the energy of youth.

We're all into smoking, having committed ourselves to that "sign of adulthood." But the hospital has strict rules about where and when we can smoke—very strict. We're always scheming for extra opportunities to smoke. The nurses can bend the rules—if they have any caring. It's such an easy thing for them to do, yet it means so much to us.

One nurse, Karen, doesn't have that simple caring, yet predictably she also has lots of power. She never gives in when it comes to the rules—she keeps strict tabs on where and when we smoke.

During Karen's shift, a few of us gather and challenge each other to go up to her to ask permission for a smoke. Nobody steps forward. Who wants to receive Karen's sarcastic rebuke which, though we've heard it many times, still manages to hurt. I volunteer. I've got a plan.

During the night I'd heard a lot of joking at the nurses' station. My bed is next to the station, and I caught a glimpse of Karen through the partly-opened door. It seemed to me she was a little drunk—more than a little drunk in fact.

I walk up to Karen, spurred on by my partners in mischief. "Karen," I say, "you know last night I had a hard time sleeping. There was a lot of noise coming from the nurses' station. Kept me awake most of the night."

"Gee, that's too bad," Karen replies. "Yeah, we had a rough time last night. That Beth, you know that nurse Beth, well she came onto the shift really loaded. We had a real hard time trying to keep her down and keep her quiet."

"Yeah," I say, "I saw all that happened. You know with my bed being right next to the nurses' station, I get a real good view of what's going on inside that station. Quite a good view."

"But you know something, Karen," I continue, being nice and friendly, "I think I'm going to forget everything I saw last night . . . "

I don't have to finish my sentence; the little power struggle is over. With a forced smile Karen methodically produces a cigarette for each of us and just as methodically she lights each one—real service. We return the smile, but ours comes from honest pleasure. It's a small victory, but then again, when you beat the system and give to yourself a bit of life, it isn't such a small victory.

The nurses dominate the atmosphere of the ward. Some make it very unpleasant. They're casually abusive. Most nurses wish only that things continue as they are. They ignore us or treat us as subhuman or stupid and perform their job with a minimum of effort. A few nurses, however, make us feel good; they introduce laughter into the ward and respect even the most bizarre and difficult patients, giving them space to be.

One nurse who makes life fun for us young girls on C-1 is Mother Eaton. She's an older woman who works on the evening shift. Mother Eaton has children of her own and treats us as though we too are her children. She really loves young people. That's how she got her name. The patients felt she was just like a mother and began calling her "mother." The name has stuck ever since. She knows how to manage us since she can be stern but kind. What energy she has! There are more than seventy patients on the ward, and she's in charge, alone. And she's like a mother to all of us.

Mother Eaton works hard to give young patients special favors. She makes us laugh and helps break the boredom by bending the rules. By letting us smoke on the wards, she violates a hospital rule—it almost costs her her job—

but it's so important to us. When I sit on the floor in the evening, smoking my cigarette and drinking a cup of coffee, I feel good, just like myself, not crazy at all.

Yes, Mother Eaton brightens many of our evenings. We wait until the supervisor finishes her rounds, and then we plug in an electric coffee pot in one of the small rooms off the ward. We look forward to having Mother Eaton join us and during these times we engage in a lot of horseplay. One time four of us tackle her onto a bed and take off her shoes and stockings and put them out on the window sill. Later that night we fill them with snow and when it comes time for her to go off duty, she has to wear a pair of hospital scuffies home. We often brag that we can handle Mother Eaton in a tussle if need be, but of course that's not true, for she always knows the best place for a whack that keeps us incorrigibles in line.

Since Mother Eaton takes care of us, we take care of her. Many of us willingly help with her ward work, cleaning and keeping things in order. And we're always making a cup of tea for her. She likes her cup of tea. And in return we get another reward—a cigarette.

One night, as Mother Eaton is standing near her desk, filling out a chart, one of the more disturbed patients leaps out of the darkness and hurls herself onto Mother Eaton, grabbing her throat. We're horrified . . . and frozen. It gets worse as Mother Eaton, unable to get away, begins to choke, and starts to turn blue. Before we can shout, I've already jumped on the girl. I start twisting her head away from Mother Eaton. Someone puts through an emergency call, and seconds later, dozens of nurses and attendants come running to the ward, pull the girl away, and release Mother Eaton. Mother Eaton loved me before, but now her love becomes deeper.

Mother Eaton is a fixture at the Castle. She grew up on the grounds because her father was in charge of the hospital farm animals—in those days the state hospitals grew most of their own food. Her grandfather also worked for the hospital and grew up on the grounds. Mother Eaton knows the Castle—inside and out. And she takes pride in the place and insists that, at least on her shift, we're treated well. She acts as if she owns the hospital—and maybe she does! Anyway, I'm so glad she's in charge of the evening shift.

Like other teenagers, we are always testing limits—our own and the hospital's. Winnie is one of our group. She's a bit retarded but is included in our activities. Winnie approaches the hospital's system differently than the rest of us. She's constantly getting into trouble for breaking rules. She gets a distinct pleasure from seeing how far she can go and willingly suffers the consequences—which is often the punishing pain of isolation or even shock treatment.

We all love Winnie; she gives us courage with her own courage. And there is no day that we're prouder of her or that made us prouder of ourselves than when an uptight psychiatrist makes his rounds of our ward, checking up on the patients, pontificating to the nurses about this patient or that and her "real" problem, treating us all like specimens on which to display his intelligence. As he enters the ward, Winnie is on her bed and begins putting her legs up in the air and kicking her feet. I look at her and say to myself, "Something is up." And then she begins hollering, "Sweet Adeline, kiss my behind," over and over again, louder and louder. The doctor tries to ignore her, though his reddening face reveals his state. But he can't make his full round of the patients and leave the ward by the other door without passing right by Winnie's bed. As he approaches her bed, she shouts with a grin, "Kiss my ass, just kiss my ass!" He accelerates his pace, walking quickly out of the ward, skipping over the remaining "specimens to be analyzed." Winnie's words trail him down the hall, "Kiss my ass, doc, kiss my blooming ass!"

Despite the fun I share with the other patients and much of the staff, the back wards are a painful and threatening reality for all of us. There are beatings in the back wards, and they are always directed toward certain patients. If the attendants want to get somebody into the seclusion room or just get back at someone who's fresh or even a little independent, they pull the person by the hair, dragging her down, kicking her. It's really upsetting to see the same patients being abused time and time again, being "picked on."

There's also the abuse that's so routine it becomes a part of living on the ward. Some of that abuse, though profoundly sad, also has its humorous side. One day the hospital supervisor comes to visit. She's observing back ward patients going through the tunnel for lunch when she notices something strange. As each patient enters through the door they duck their head—even though the doorway is a normal institutional ten foot height.

"Why are they all ducking?" she asks curiously.

We all have to laugh, knowing no one would tell her the real version. Every day—except the day of her visit—a big, strapping nurse is stationed at the doorway with a large metal soup ladle, banging each and every patient on the head as they enter for food. The crack on the head—more than a little tap mind you—is intended to establish order in the cafeteria. Patients can't talk or do anything but eat in the cafeteria, and the crack on the head is a little reminder of that rule. Some patients are continually acting out on the back ward—the soup ladle "quiets" them down!

Several of us young patients begin laughing at the supervisor as she tries to understand the dance of ducking heads performed before her—without the essential ingredient. She never figures it out—no one gives her the missing clue of the soup ladle. It's funny even to us who know what it feels like to be hit three times a day just in order to eat. But I'm also thinking to myself, "What's a hit on the head compared to the other punishments around here?"

Even more abusive is the way a nurse will sometimes provoke and antagonize chronic patients just because she's bored. One nurse in particular is unforgivably cruel in this way. There is one patient, Carol, who's really sick. The nurse yells at Carol, taunts her, and then orders her to put her feces all over the wall. Carol becomes enraged, and she and the nurse begin yelling back and forth at each other. But the nurse always prevails, and yelling fiercely at Carol, makes her smear her feces on the wall—and then makes her clean it all up! Just so the nurse won't be bored.

It doesn't take much to be sent to a back ward. Just smoking after eleven in the evening can be sufficient cause. I always live in fear of the back wards. I can count on being there by the end of a week if I'm not careful. Not all the attendants are like Mother Eaton; many are cruel and have no liking for young people, considering us no more than spoiled brats. I spend a lot of time on the back wards for violations of the many hospital rules; and I'm always frightened when I'm there, fearing I'll be kept there forever. This fear remains with me still, and when I think of the back wards chills shake me.

One day, as I'm mopping the floor on C-1, I hear the lower door open and notice that a female patient is being brought into the ward in a wheelchair. "She's being taken to B-1, the admission ward," I think to myself and go on mopping. As the attendant approaches the door leading out of our ward, I look at the woman sitting in the wheelchair—she looks familiar. She's thin, disheveled, and appears "out of it."

"Is that one your mother?" one of the patients asks me, pointing to the wheelchair. The question stuns me. I look again at the woman and can't believe what I see. I don't know what to do—there's my mother! I later hear that the other patient had learned that my mother was being admitted, but said nothing to prepare me for that fact. I'm struck by her cruelty; the patient seemed to be trying to hurt me.

I recognize my mother—it doesn't seem she recognizes me. Walking away bewildered, without saying a word to my mother or to anyone else, I go to the sunporch and sit, unable to make sense of things. It becomes even more confusing when I learn that my mother is taken not to B-1, the admissions ward, but to A-2, the back ward.

For the first few days I say nothing about my mother being admitted to the back ward and no one mentions it to me. I'm angry. My mother's drinking, which led to my own most recent admission to the Castle, causes me to resent her. When she finally is brought to C-1, where I am, I swallow my pride, suppress my anger, and speak to her. Though I try to be kind, I find it difficult. Having her on the same ward is too much—it makes my decision to leave inevitable. Eventually I build up enough courage to contact Ma and Pa Bartello. All the while they've been calling the hospital doctor to find out how I'm doing. They've sent messages saying that they want to see me. Now I call them and Ma answers the phone—we both just start to cry. I say nothing about my mother being at the Castle. I'm too ashamed. Pa gets on the phone and I continue to cry bitterly to him, asking him to come for me. He says he'll see that I'm home by the next day, and, true to his word, I am. Ma comes for me and I'm signed out against medical advice. I've been at the Castle for one year during this most recent admission. I'm already used to coming and going from the Castle, and say my good-byes before leaving with Ma.

I still have the same haunting fear of Pa and have to get used to his rigid, stern personality, but the two months that I remain with Ma and Pa are uneventful. I never divulge to them that my mother was admitted to the Castle and I never discuss my own life at the Castle, though I'm sure they must wonder what it has been like. Though I have a few minor arguments with Ma while Pa is away fishing, most of the time things go smoothly—but I'm not happy. I'm able to look only outside of myself for happiness, constantly avoiding any search inside.

One day, as I'm sitting at the kitchen table with Ma and Pa, the telephone rings. I answer it. My sister Gerry is calling and I sense almost immediately that something is wrong.

"There's been a fire," Gerry's voice speeds along to its devastating conclusion. "And mother, well, mother is in bad shape. She's in the hospital . . . and they don't think she'll live."

We exchange a few more words, and I learn that mother had been discharged from the Castle before the accident. After getting the local hospital address, I put the phone down—I'm in a fog. Feeling desperate, I turn to Ma and Pa and tell them about the fire and my mother's terrible condition.

"I have to go to my mother and see her in the hospital," I tell them. The next few moments are full of tension, anxiety, and guilt.

"You shouldn't go!" Pa insists. "That woman isn't even your mother. Ma is your mother." His voice has become angry.

I feel an urgency to leave quickly, yet I'm very confused. Who is my mother? I'm torn. "I have two mothers," I say simply to Pa, hoping to blunt his anger. "I've got to go to the mother that needs me the most," I continue. It's my place to go, for I had left mother with anger and rejection and I don't want to neglect her now. Pa's eyes become moist—then wet with tears. I feel horribly guilty, but there's no more I can say. I pack my suitcase and leave.

Mother had fallen asleep while smoking in bed and her nightgown had caught on fire. She was almost completely ablaze, leaving her with third degree burns over two-thirds of her body. My grandmother, who was bedridden with a broken hip, called from her bed for a neighbor who came rushing into the apartment. My grandmother yelled to the neighbor to get a blanket and throw it over my mother who was burning alive, but the neighbor disregarded my grandmother's pleas. Instead, she threw a bucket of water over my mother who finally collapsed into unconsciousness. This is what my sister Gerry tells me as we sit in the hospital foyer.

In the hospital room my mother is lying there, still and unconscious. Her face is beet red and a crib with a sheet on it is placed over her, protecting her ravaged body. I try to speak to her but there is no response. I tell Gerry that I'll stay with mother until it's over. Mother lives twenty days and dies quietly. As I sit in the church listening to the priest celebrate the Mass for the dead, I feel dead inside; all emotion is gone. My anger is buried so deep that it doesn't emerge until many years later. That night, dry-eyed, I leave the cemetery and go back to the Castle. I'm twenty-one. I've lasted on the "outside" for only two months.

7. "Treatments"

*T*he hospital staff is angry with me for coming back to the Castle so soon. I hear the whispering voices of a couple of attendants, "Oh, she's back again! Just look at her, that little kid couldn't make it." I'm embarrassed and wish there's someplace I can just go to hide. I feel like a failure, even though I know there's no place else for me to go after the terrible loss of my mother. If I tell staff what has happened, I'm sure many of them will be more sympathetic but it's too painful to talk about. Besides, I know my mother is now gone for good. I can't see how it will help to talk about her. I'm angry with my mother for dying, but at the same time, I want to protect her from having the image of an irresponsible and destructive alcoholic.

Though there are a lot of negative feelings toward me, the positive attitude of many make living at the Castle more than just tolerable. Before long I'm a trusted patient and have access to different areas of the hospital. Some nurses take me to the various wards when they have errands to do, and often I have the freedom of the hospital grounds.

That doesn't mean that I don't see my share of the back wards for I'm always "acting out"—and then I'm sent there. One day, I become angry with the nurse in charge of the ward because she won't allow me to have a cigarette. She insists that there will be no smoking until all the ward work is done. I deliberately run up to the window at the end of the ward and smash it with my fist. I can feel the sharp pain from the impact but don't realize how badly I am cut. A barrage of nurses, about six of them, come running down to where I am standing and grab me. Blood is over all of us. They take me to the treatment room where a doctor sutures my hand and then march me off to A-2, the back ward. I try to break away from their grip as they drag me up the stairs, but I don't have the strength to match their combined force. They strip off my clothing and throw me into the seclusion room. A few minutes later, three nurses come into the room, one of them carrying a large syringe. They hold me down as I fight like a cornered animal, give me a shot, and leave me alone, lying on the mattress. That time I remain on the back ward only two days.

Perhaps the most tragic thing that I see on the wards involves a young woman named Rita. She's really having a hard time. She has four children and misses them terribly. Rita's feeling sick—hearing voices which are relentless in their accusation. I sit with her on her bed, and she cries and cries, wishing for relief from her voices, wishing to see her children. Rita's a really attractive woman and she desperately wants to get better to be reunited with her kids. But the staff doesn't understand her. They think she's faking the voices and because she isn't getting any better, they believe she isn't doing anything to help herself. Rita needs help! Instead, in their ignorance and anger, they send Rita to the worst of the back wards where only the chronic catatonics and delusional clients are, where clients are half-dressed at best.

I go up to the back ward whenever I can and sit with Rita. She looks so lost. "How can they do this to her!? It's not right, they're killing her," I think as we visit, and try not to break into tears. It tears me to pieces to see her there and to see her gradually deteriorate over the months. Her beauty is etched away by her pain and hopelessness. No one cares for her . . . and she has ceased caring for herself. Rita goes completely downhill and is cut off from me. Soon she's like the other tragic figures on the back ward. I can't keep going anymore—it hurts me too much. What Rita suffers is crueler, more painful than any beating. Fortunately she recovers somehow and finally is released from the hospital.

As the months go by, my friendship with Mother Eaton and Miss Harris, the head nurse on C-1, deepens. I feel very close to them both. Miss Harris and I sneak down to the tunnel, where the dirty laundry is stored, to sit on the stairway and smoke, since she isn't allowed to smoke on the ward. During these moments, I feel trusted and accepted as a real person. My self-esteem rises sharply when I think she chose me to go there with her! Yet I'm still like a child with her, having no intention of changing or growing up.

Though I'm not considered very sick mentally, I don't go without treatment. But many "treatments" feel more like punishments—and the nurses use them punitively. At one point I'm given shock treatments, which I really dread. I can never forget the electrodes smeared with jelly and joined together with a rubber band. The worst is the moment when the electrodes are placed on my temples while the doctor pushes the little button on the black box. It's physically painless, but the idea of being sent into unconsciousness by an electric shock gives me a terrible fear of the unknown. It's like drowning while I'm still alive, suffocating on my own loss of thoughts, being filled with dark, black cotton. I don't submit to this treatment willingly—the nurses have to drag me to the "shock room." Once I hide under a bed thinking they won't find me until the treatments are over. Another time I intentionally eat a whole breakfast thinking that they surely won't give me shock treatment, since you need an empty stomach for the treatments. Eating all that food is awful. Before I'd never been able to keep down even a careful selection of food from any other meal, as the food is always disgusting to me. But the treatment schedule prevails—in I go with a full stomach!

At the time sodium pentathol was not used as it is today, so I'm *awake* during the whole procedure, fully aware of the little black box with the button, the button that sends electricity through my body. Seeing the doctor at the button, I feel suspended in a pool of terror as I wait to be dropped under water, out of consciousness. After treatment I wonder if the attending doctors ever think of themselves as the "one who pushes the button" or whether they just take that action for granted as part of their work. In total I have twelve shock treatments, and I'm so relieved when I survive the last one.

There are several other forms of therapy used at the Castle which are today outmoded because of the present use of psychotropic drugs or tranquilizers. Sub-Insulin Therapy is one, but it does no more for me than add twenty pounds to my one hundred and two. The insulin is injected into a vein in my arm, and within a few minutes I fall into a semicomatose state, deeply unconscious. I don't think the staff understands the terrors of those treatments in which a patient passes out. With each treatment I feel I'm dying; and with insulin therapy, it's a slow death. Each time I'm convinced I won't live through the treatment. When I wake up I perspire so profusely that I feel like a drenched rat. The treatment lasts about four hours. There seems to be one advantage to the treatments: I'm put on a special diet, which is a little better than that served to the rest of the hospital population.

Two other forms of treatments are conducted in the Hydro-Therapy Department: "tubs" and "wet packs." Each lasts most of the day beginning at eight in the morning and ending at four in the afternoon with a one hour lunch break at noon. In "tubs" I'm placed in a huge bathtub filled with hot water at a constant temperature and covered with a canvas top. My head sticks through a hole at one end of the canvas. I'm completely covered by the canvas—all you can see is my head bobbing back and forth. This treatment is given to calm me down when I'm acting up, and it does have a soothing effect.

"Wet packs," on the other hand, are not as "pleasant." Sheets are immersed in ice cold water and then wrapped completely around me except for my head. When I'm in the "pack" I'm like a mummy. This treatment is usually used on the more disturbed patients but is also used as a means of punishment. When lying in a "wet pack" I feel very cold at first, but then my body temperature warms me. When I'm removed at the end of the day, I feel very light in head and body, and much calmer. But being wrapped tightly in these sheets all day is torture. During the treatments, patients are constantly screaming and swearing. I can't stand their painful and angry cries, but I can't do anything about it, immobilized as I am in my own sheet. I feel like I'm going crazy as their horrible screams penetrate me, their voices drilling holes into my skull.

The wet packs have a particularly abusive variation. The nurses grab you and throw a wet sheet over you that's rubbed with lye soap. They put the sheet right over your head so you begin to gag. I go through this punishment more times than I really want to remember. I gag, and gasp for air, sucking in that horrible lye soap smell, and gasp and gasp for less and less of the smelly air, and then feel the terror of no longer being able to breathe anything. It's then that I black out—or so I'm told!

I can avoid going to "wet packs" if I want to. But I'm barely a teenager emotionally—even though I'm nearly twenty-two. I seek some independence and naturally I'm a bit rebellious; at times, I act like a spoiled brat. All of these tentative, and for me, awkward, attempts toward developmental maturity lead into trouble. One night I get into a heated argument with the evening nurse because she insists on my being in bed at ten o'clock. I don't feel sleepy so I refuse and remain sitting in a chair listening to the radio. I have earplugs so I believe it's OK—the noise isn't disturbing anyone. But I'm breaking a rule and also being disrespectful to the nurse in charge. The next morning I'm sent to "packs."

Though I have many problems during this time in the Castle, such as my depression, my inability to express anger, and my "acting out" behavior, I don't want to "get better." I know I can control my acting out if I make the effort, but I'm afraid that if I behave as the staff wants me to, I'll be discharged. I'm comfortable at the hospital and don't want to risk living in the "outside" world where I'd be unable to make a life for myself. Wanting to remain in the Castle, I avoid or ignore the periodic efforts staff make to help—the caring questions about my feelings, the encouragement to think about leaving, and the several attempts to engage me in a kind of brief psychotherapy.

Ma visits me at the Castle whenever she can, always asking me to go back home. She's seventy-two now, and it's increasingly difficult for her to make the trip. Each time she brings a shopping bag full of sandwiches, boxes of cookies, and all sorts of fresh fruit. I start looking forward to her visits but feel guilty for not going home with her. One particular day, however, she starts crying, pleading with me to return with her. Resisting her pleas is more difficult than in the past—and I agree to go. She's very happy and a short time later comes back with an Italian woman to interpret for her and make arrangements with the doctor. Within thirty minutes I'm reluctantly leaving the Castle, where I've been for the past year, and returning to Gloucester. It's winter.

Though it's cold, the familiar houses along the narrow streets of Gloucester give me the good feeling of being home. Our house looks the same with its large windows and big porch in the front. It's high tide and the waves are edging close to the fence that protects our lawn. I like the strong salty air though the winter ocean is forboding. For a brief moment I put the Castle out of my mind, but somewhere deep inside, I miss all the people there.

My first two weeks home go by fast. I help Ma clean the house and do all the shopping. Ginger, my best friend, comes over often. She's fun to be with and we rehash old times. She's sympathetic towards me and understands how unhappy and mixed up I feel.

Pa is down in Mississippi fishing and not expected home until the end of winter. He calls every two weeks or so. One afternoon, Ma, a neighbor, and I are sitting in the kitchen, talking. Instinctively I turn to the window. I can't believe what I see! Pa is coming towards the house. He walks in and we all greet him. His face is rosy from the cold air, and he appears in good health though he's thinner than I remember. Taking off his hat and coat, he walks toward the kitchen table. As he comes closer, I go up to him to give him a kiss when he suddenly slips into the chair. He throws his head back and slumps sideways. I see his eyes roll back into his head and call out to him, "Pa . . . Pa!" He never answers. Pa is dead.

It's impossible for me to think of Pa as dead. His personality was so overpowering he seemed indestructible. He was always a physically strong man and never had anything seriously wrong with him. In my mind, nothing could destroy Pa or take him away for good—not even God.

During the rest of the afternoon, people come in and out of the house trying to console Ma, who has gone to pieces. That evening I go next door to Ginger's house and spend the night. As I lie on the bed in the dark, a strange feeling creeps over me. I'm terrified! Fear takes hold of me in the pit of my stomach and my head feels as though it will burst from the pressure rising inside. I begin shaking and shuddering in uncontrollable waves. I'm so scared, scared that I'm going crazy. I don't know what is happening. Then, as the shuddering continues, I begin vomiting and dry retching. I'm afraid I'm going to die. Fear just pours over me—into my head and into my heart. If God could take Pa, surely He can take me. Any moment now I'll be overtaken by an awful death. I'm afraid to fall asleep because I'm afraid I'll never wake up. Morning takes so long to come as I stay awake the entire night, lying stiffly on the bed, in terror.

In the morning I feel better, glad the night is finally over. I get up very early and go back to the house to see Ma who has also had a bad night. Relatives have stayed with her and arrangements have already been made for the wake and funeral. It's Ma's wish that Pa be waked at home. I had hoped she wouldn't do that for it means that people will be constantly coming to the house throughout the day and night, and we won't get any rest. But it's the traditional way and Ma insists on having Pa's body brought to the house.

All during the wake and throughout the funeral that haunting fear creeps up on me, and I use all my energy to keep it in check. I'm so consumed by this anxiety that I spend all of my time coping with it rather than dealing with the grief that is buried deep inside me. I feel all fear and no loss. My Pa's dead; he won't come back. I know I should cry for him, but instead I do nothing but feel threatened by my own imminent death and destruction. Often I want to scream, but I don't want to create a bad scene so I make a concerted effort to be in control at all times. It means using every bit of my physical and emotional energy, leaving me totally drained. I don't tell anyone how badly I really feel because I'm afraid they'll say I've gone stark mad. Besides, I figure what's really important is to maintain my self-control—and eventually these intense feelings will go away. They never do.

I've learned from recent psychiatric consultation that I was suffering from acute panic attacks—attacks which plagued me for years.

My brother Marco and sister-in-law Sarah come up from Mississippi for the funeral. They had gone there to live while Marco worked with Pa on his fishing boat. After the funeral the estate is settled promptly. There isn't much left because Pa had suffered a financial setback several years before. Ma's upset because he left so little. And then it becomes clear—Ma is also upset with me.

At first, I can't understand Ma's change of attitude toward me. She always professes her love for me to others, but now she can't stand my being home with her anymore. Maybe I'm too much of a burden for her. She's in need of financial as well as emotional support, and maybe she sees me as too weak to fulfill these needs of hers. Anyway, she makes arrangements for me to leave for Mississippi with Sarah. I agree, thinking that perhaps a new life in a different part of the country might be just what I need. About three weeks after the funeral, I fly to Mississippi with high hopes for a better future.

The move to Mississippi is difficult. I'm running away from my problems—and they follow me. Overwhelming attacks of fear still come with no warning. I make an honest effort to keep these feelings suppressed, but they are controlling my life; it's becoming more and more difficult to function. I see a doctor who prescribes a mild tranquilizer, but when it doesn't help I stop taking it.

I remain with Sarah, Marco, and their four children for several months but finally leave because I can't get along with them. I'm short tempered and tense most of the time, and they have a hard time adjusting to my mood swings. I decide to go to Mobile, Alabama, and try to get a job. When I arrive there I check the telephone directory, looking for work in a hospital, and get a job in an orphanage affiliated with a large general hospital. I work with the newborn babies and live in the nurses' quarters.

After working at the orphanage for almost a year, I get a higher paying job with a doctor who needs office help, and move to the Y.W.C.A. I like the new job and enjoy living at the "Y" where I make friends with several of the residents. But I'm still having anxiety attacks that interfere with my job. I begin thinking of going home to Gloucester. Ma doesn't want me back, but maybe she'll at least let me in the house temporarily. I'm not sure why I don't think of going back to the Castle, but I'm only trying to survive the attacks that are crippling me, and maybe my home in Gloucester will provide the needed support. Returning home, I'm a twenty-six-year-old woman still very much the child, instinctively seeking safety and shelter from her Ma.

8. *The Outside World*

*T*he train pulls into Gloucester—it's nearly 7:00 P.M. As the sharp, February wind fills the open station door, it chills me since I'm still dressed in the summer clothes I've worn in Alabama. My friend Ginger meets me at the station and has a taxi waiting to take us home. Glad to see each other, we talk excitedly, trying to catch up with the past year's happenings in five minutes. Before I realize it, I'm standing at Ma's front door. I know she's home because I saw her sitting at the kitchen window as we drove past in the taxi. Calling out to her, I knock several times but she won't answer. I'm hurt, feeling like a stray dog who doesn't deserve to be lost. I've come a long way, it's cold, and I'm tired. Sure, Ma doesn't want to have anything more to do with me, but she shouldn't turn me away with no place to go. I'm getting angrier and angrier. After several more attempts to get her to open the door, I finally give up and leave.

Ginger has already gone home. The only place I can think of going is to cousin Lena's. As I walk to her house, my insides are trembling from the cold. The ten minute walk seems like an hour. Lena and her family are really glad to see me and in just a few minutes I'm eating a bowl of hot soup, telling them about my attempt to get Ma to let me in. Lena doesn't have enough room at her house, so she arranges for me to stay with another cousin, Anna. Since Anna is close to Ma it's felt that perhaps she can get Ma to come to her senses—Anna seldom loses an argument. Overtired from the long trip and very worried, I can't sleep even though I go to bed early. Although I could have easily gone back to the Castle, it doesn't enter my mind.

The following morning there's a knock at the door. It's Ma. I leave the room so that Anna can talk to her privately. I think Ma has already made up her mind that she'll take me home because it doesn't take Anna long to convince her. I overhear Anna telling Ma that I belong at home and that both of us need each other. After a few minutes I join them, telling Ma that I'll try not to be a burden to her and try to help her. Ma seems satisfied and I can feel the tension in the room evaporate.

I spend two stormy years at home with Ma. I try holding a job in a frozen fish factory, but because of my continuing attacks of anxiety, I have to quit after three weeks. To make matters worse, Ma's health, now that she's in her late seventies, is failing rapidly. She's too old and too sick to cope with a twenty-six-year-old daughter who's grown so dependent on her.

Because of her age, Ma has also become very forgetful and although I do nothing to engender her mistrust, she always feels I'm taking advantage of her. She'll hide money, forget where she's hidden it, and then accuse me of taking it. And when she's found it again, she doesn't apologize. One day she loses a five dollar gold piece which she's always worn around her neck on a gold chain. She hunts and hunts for it but can't find it. She becomes so upset that she complains to a neighbor that I've stolen it. This gets back to me. I'm so angry that I start to scream at Ma. I'm finding it harder and harder to be patient with her. More and more I'm losing my temper and screaming at her. Then I feel guilty because I've yelled at an old woman. Ma finds her gold piece a week later. Having broken loose from her neck, it had slipped beneath the sofa cushions. She never apologizes.

What makes living with Ma especially difficult is that she's so far removed from my generation. She doesn't allow me to date or bring home friends, male or female. The only friend she approves of is Ginger and that's because Ginger doesn't date but stays at home and takes care of her elderly father. I want to have friends but because of Ma's attitude, most of the young women I know tend to stay away. Also, many of my friends are already married—our interests have grown apart.

Although living with Ma is filled with problems, it's difficult to move out. I feel totally unequipped to live independently. I can't hold down a job because of severe anxiety attacks and increasing depression. Also I've no particular skills with which to start a career. I've been sheltered all my life. Pa believed that women should not have to support themselves, so at an early age I learned to depend on others for my support. Another obstacle to going out on my own is my fear that I can't handle myself emotionally. Because of the time I've spent at the Castle, others treat me as someone who'll never be able to stand on her own feet—I guess I believe them.

During my last year with Ma, she starts to complain that she isn't feeling well. She visits the doctor frequently, but he can't diagnose what's ailing her. On Thanksgiving Day, we eat a turkey dinner brought to us by one of our relatives.

Shortly after she's eaten, Ma begins to vomit. After I clean up the mess, I bathe her, help her into her nightgown, and put her to bed. By nighttime her condition worsens and I telephone the doctor. After he examines her, he calls an ambulance and within the hour, Ma is on her way to Gloucester General Hospital.

She's in the hospital for fourteen days and during that time I feel completely torn apart and abandoned. I visit her every day and each time she looks worse. Often a nurse calls on the phone, "Your ma's asking for you. I think you should come back to see her." Finally Ma goes into a coma. The doctor says she has diabetes and that there's no chance of survival. Seeing her is torment. Her face has the look of death, and when I return home in the evening, I expect any minute to hear she's gone. The phone rings often, but it's always a neighbor or relative inquiring about Ma. Each time after I hang up the phone, I dash for the toilet and vomit. I'm so frightened that at one point I cry out to God for help. I can't express what I want to say. Words just burst out, unconnected, "God, help . . . I'm scared . . . help me . . . " But there is no help. Death finally comes to Ma and I'm alone. My last bit of hope dies with her and I cry all night.

Ma is waked at the funeral home and then buried alongside of Pa. During the wake my head hurts—it's like a fever. I try to ignore it but by the time of the funeral I feel so bad I can't go. My relatives understand and don't pressure me. While the funeral is taking place, I'm at cousin Anna's. Conflicting thoughts about what's in store for me make me confused. Now I can't think of my future—there is none.

Shortly after noon, Anna returns with a few of the relatives. I'm very tense as we all sit at the kitchen table discussing the funeral. Anna prepares lunch and soon we're busy eating cold meat sandwiches with cheese and sliced tomatoes. I'm not very hungry but try to eat anyway. When lunch is over we clear the table and prepare for the hot coffee perking on the stove. As I sit next to Anna, an overwhelming attack of anxiety hits me without warning. I want to run as fast as I can but struggle to keep my legs still. They begin to twitch. I remain sitting at the table—about to lose control. Finally I speak up. "I'm really not feeling well," my voice cracks with panic. " . . . I've got to go home now . . . I need some rest."

As soon as I reach the street, I run as fast as I can. My very life depends on reaching Ma's house. The tension in my head is at the boiling point, and as I pass the cars on the road, they fade before my eyes. The sidewalk is thin air under my racing feet and appears to be tipped sideways, making me unsteady. There's the house! I can't believe I've made it. Out of breath, my heart pounding wildly, I run up the stairs, swing open the door, and race to my room. There's the bed! I throw myself on it.

Lying there, I close my eyes. The intense pressure in my head frightens me—I'm afraid my blood vessels are going to burst. I try to calm myself, telling myself over and over, "Everything's going to be all right. Just don't give in to this . . . I can't give in to this." I slowly open my eyes and as I gaze about the room, I feel death all about me. The room tilts at an angle and while I stare straight ahead, it becomes distorted, as if a shiny window has been placed directly in front of my eyes. Everything is confusing—I lose my bearings and no longer know what I'm doing. Around me everything is slipping away and I reach for something, anything, but there's nothing to hang on to. Am I going crazy? Or am I dying? I don't know whether

I'm insane or dying—I've never experienced this before
. . . and I'm really scared!

All the while, as I try to control myself, I'm struggling
to stay alive. The panic in my stomach mounts and recedes
like a moving tide—it's got to stop! I think of Ma's sleeping pills. In desperation, I dash into the bathroom. My
head's reeling back and forth. The floor's rolling under my
feet. Here's a bottle of sleeping capsules on the top shelf of
the medicine cabinet—I'm relieved. I take one capsule with
a glass of water and go back to bed. Soon I'm asleep but
still restless and tense.

When I open my eyes I look about the room to see what
it's like. Everything is in place and the room is no longer
tilted. I'm a little hung over from the sleeping pill and my
head is fuzzy. But the sleep has helped. I'm no longer so
panic stricken, though my stomach is still queasy. It's dark
now, though the moonlight makes the room with all its
furnishings clearly visible. Turning on the lamp, I look
at the clock. I'm surprised—it's eight o'clock. I've slept
four hours.

My head still aches and my body feels hot. The terrible
experience of a few hours earlier must have been emotional
because I'm still alive, but maybe I'm physically sick as
well. I take my temperature—104°. That's OK. But I still
feel the grip of that terrible upheaval, even though I'm
calmer. I must be mentally sick—and that terrifying
upheaval will soon repeat itself.

What should I do next? I don't want to disturb my
relatives—they won't understand, or even care. But I can't
stay in the house—death is still there. I'd better leave the
house and go to the hotel which is only a few minutes'
walk away. I pack a few clothes and leave.

Once in the hotel room, I lie down on the bed and wrap myself in blankets. Racked by chills, I can't get warm. As my whole body shivers, the panic in my stomach twists my insides and makes me sick. I start to vomit. Trying not to soil the rugs I grab a wastebasket. I continue to vomit until after midnight. Between bouts of sickness I cry in desperation, crying out for someone to hold me. Immobilized by fear, I see no way out. The only thing to do is to call my family doctor. At 1:00 A.M. I'm reluctant to wake her up but I need help. I phone. A sleepy voice answers and I tell Dr. Evert about Ma's death and how sick I feel emotionally as well as physically. She admits me to Gloucester General Hospital and within a half-hour I'm there. A nurse helps me to bed and gives me a shot. I begin relaxing and soon I'm sleeping. I'm glad to be where I can get some help.

When I wake up the next morning I'm relieved to find the symptoms of yesterday have subsided. The hospital gives me a sense of security which I'd totally lost when Ma died. With Ma gone, there's no one left to care for me, no one who's concerned about what will happen to me.

I've never felt completely accepted by the Bartello relatives—I'm "in the way" as far as they're concerned. Although my sister-in-law Sarah and brother Marco are living in the area again and are willing to have me stay with them, this can be only a short-term solution. The thought of being responsible for myself overwhelms me. I'm so insecure and ill-equipped to handle my future, and I know the emotional distress of yesterday will recur . . . and then I can't control those feelings. I feel hopeless.

I'm very surprised when, two days later, the doctor tells me I have mononucleosis and infectious hepatitis. My first reaction is that I've enough problems without any further complications. The doctor explains that I need bedrest and a proper diet, but I don't pay much attention to her instructions. I'm concerned about what can be done for my mental condition, and when the doctor orders me a tranquilizer, I relax a bit.

When Sarah comes to see me I repeat to her what the doctor has said but mention nothing about my distressing emotional experiences. She agrees to take me home with her, at least temporarily, until I can decide what I want to do. Although I don't want to be any trouble to Sarah and Marco, I go home with them—it's the only thing I can do at that time. I want very much to put the pieces of my life together, but I don't believe that I'm equal to the task.

Leaving Gloucester General, I feel very shaky. My first day at Sarah's is a quiet one. She makes some chicken soup for supper, and, after spending the afternoon in bed, I'm able to eat. I'm making sense when I talk and I look pretty good physically. But all the while I'm struggling inside. The panic still seems imminent, ready to overwhelm me again. Yet I manage to get through the day.

Making it through the day is one thing but the night brings another round of torment. Lying in bed in the quiet house, I hear the heavy breathing of the children as they sleep. Then, the panic slowly mounts and I hide my head under the covers so that I don't scream out. I'm lost! Crying, slowly at first, and then uncontrollably, I try to pray but the words stick in my mind and I can't go on. Suddenly, I feel that I have to get out. I'm desperate to flee, but where should I go? The Loring General in Boston. They have an emergency care ward. This time I'm really sick and surely they'll help me. I quietly dress, grab my winter jacket, and sneak out of the house. I can't make any sense out of what I'm doing; I just have to get away.

At 12:00 in the morning the last train to Boston pulls into the Gloucester station. I board and go directly to a seat. When the train begins to move, I seize the arms of my seat with a tight grip. I feel drawn upward—my body sucked into the door and out the moving train. I sit rigidly in total terror. The conductor approaches and asks for my fare. I try to hide my distress by smiling. When I finally accomplish the purchase of my ticket, and the conductor moves on to the next seat, I take several easy breaths, but the relief is temporary. As the train makes its various stops, I sit as if glued to my seat. My hands, now sweaty, are stiff from the force of my grip. I'm too terrified to move even a slight bit. The only way I can stop myself from jumping off the train is to hold on to my seat for dear life. It's only an hour's ride to Boston, but the train seems to go on and on, stopping slowly, so slowly, at each town on the way. When, finally, the conductor calls out, "Boston!" I relax slightly and quickly step down the platform. Walking out to the street, I hail a taxi to take me to the hospital.

I'm standing in front of the emergency entrance of Loring General. It's nearly 2:00 A.M. and a strong west wind is blowing. The cold air sharpens my senses—it feels good to be able to think a little more clearly. After a few moments, I enter. A nurse directs me to a small examining room and tells me to wait. I'm starting to settle down. I wait nervously for the doctor to arrive and when he does, I begin sobbing unashamedly, letting go of my bound-up anxiety.

Dr. Green is a tall, middle-aged man. I feel uneasy as he looks down at me with his penetrating eyes. He asks what's troubling me as I try to wipe away my tears.

"I don't know . . . I don't know what's really wrong with me," I struggle to explain what I've been experiencing since Ma's death but I'm awkward under his steady gaze, and I can't find the words to describe the panic attacks.

Dr. Green is impatient—he wants some answers.

"I've got mononucleosis and hepatitis. They told me that at Loring." It seems easier to start with my physical problems. "But I have other problems that I'm really afraid of . . . feelings that scare me like I've never been scared before . . . they come suddenly . . . I'm so frightened I want to run away, for my life . . . " I'm not making much sense but that's the best I can do. It's too difficult to express what I really feel.

Dr. Green looks at me, but I know he's not interested. Perhaps if I had described my mental condition more clearly, he could understand my desperation. But these panic attacks are new experiences for me—I have a hard time describing them even to myself and Dr. Green doesn't encourage me to find the necessary words.

Although I've been in the mental hospital before, this is the first time I've felt more than just depressed. I'd seen plenty of other patients at Sutton State who were seriously ill but I didn't realize then that they might be suffering from the same kind of feelings that I've just had. I didn't realize then the pain they must be suffering. I try to convince Dr. Green that I'm desperate, fragile, and anxious, that I'm having the hallucinations of a mental patient . . . that I'm mentally ill. But he disregards everything I tell him, and considering only my physical condition, admits me to the emergency medical ward. I remain there for three days while tests are completed to verify the diagnosis of mononucleosis and hepatitis. Then Dr. Green wants to discharge me. But when he realizes that I definitely won't return to Gloucester, he sends a hospital social worker to talk to me about going to a nursing home to recuperate physically. The social worker listens attentively as I explain why I don't want to go to a nursing home—they're too gloomy and depressing. She assures me she'll find a suitable place and within two days she is driving me to Crestwood Manor.

I'm very unsure about going to Crestwood but agree because it seems to be the only place available. At least I'll be secure there and that's important. I figure that if I'm secure I can be relatively free from my emotional problems—that's what happened in my recent stays at Gloucester General Hospital and Loring General.

Crestwood is located on the outskirts of Boston, across from a beautiful park. The building itself is an attractive home which has recently been renovated. The place doesn't have the usual nursing home smell—I'm glad. A nurse greets me, taking me into a three-bed room that's occupied by two older women who are both confined to wheelchairs. She introduces me to my two new roommates and then, after a few words of reassurance, leaves.

Though its rooms are light and its furnishings new, Crestwood still has an atmosphere of hopelessness. The other patients are very old—my two roommates have little hope of leaving Crestwood alive. There's little to amuse me in Crestwood. There's no radio or T.V. in my room, and I'm not allowed in other parts of the house. I begin to feel restless and depressed. Some of my old anxiety returns and I try to cope with it by taking long walks in the park.

Before the first week is over, I'm thinking of leaving Crestwood and confide my intention of running away to my roommates. I still have the uneasy feeling that my emotional problem is not completely gone. Although I've had no severe panic attacks recently, I still feel sick—anxious and depressed. I can't return to Gloucester—my relatives don't want to have to put up with me. So I decide that my only alternative is to go back to the Castle. I've been away four years—I've remained in the "outside world" as long as I can. One day I pack my suitcase, say good-bye to my roommates and sneak out of Crestwood. I walk toward the subway station, knowing I'm leaving that "outside world" and won't return for a long time.

9. Back Ward

"Oh she's back again. We knew she couldn't make it!" That's what I expect to hear from the staff on my return to the Castle. In deciding to come back I anticipate the cynicism of the staff and their disappointment when patients go into crisis or fail to achieve their goals—and I don't want to confront those attitudes. But, I'm surprised. Actually the staff on B-1 is quite pleased that I've managed to stay outside for four years. Several of the nurses who were there during my earlier admissions even welcome me back, like an old-timer, making me feel as if I've come back to friends.

They explain that B-1 has changed since my last discharge. It's now used for admissions and for the younger patients, who are coming to the Castle in far greater numbers. B-1 is no longer filled with incontinent, half-naked old ladies, who are now being housed in their own ward. B-1 looks better—there's a fresh coat of yellow paint and more furniture around. And it feels better—the younger patients are more lively and able to carry on a conversation. It's really nice to see the familiar faces of some of the more helpful staff, though there are also many new staff as well. I'm at home soon after arriving.

I'm feeling pretty good, especially since the anxiety and turmoil which has recently flooded my life seems behind me now. There's another surprise—the dreaded shock treatments, as well as the hot tubs and insulin therapies, are no more. Just thinking about those shock treatments—which I try not to do—makes me shiver and sweat, and feel dizzy. When I hear that they're no longer used, I'm even more sure that I've come back to the right place.

But the admission process scares me this time in a new and different way. I know the routine; that doesn't bother me. But something ominous is happening.

"Tell me what you've been doing since your last admission." The admitting attendant's question is matter-of-fact and predictable. But where other times on admission my answers were brief or nonexistent, this time, I want to say a lot. I talk about Pa and Ma's deaths, and all the terrible emotions I experienced from them. I really work at explaining how I feel, saying over and over that I've never been so scared in my life as I describe being overwhelmed by frightening distortions and the racing, whirling jumble of my mind.

The attendant looks at me while I talk and doesn't interrupt. She looks at me and listens, but I know she's not grasping what I'm saying. That frightens me even more. I desperately want her to realize that things are not the same as before. I'm not just a lost, confused, and depressed youngster, as I had been on my last admission. Now I'm trying to cope with something far different, a real mental sickness, and I need help very badly. Though the intensity of the recent emotional turmoil has receded, it's still seething inside me, ready to bust out. I want help, but at the same time I don't want to get so well that I might have to leave the hospital. The attendant's blank look gives me nothing—it's the same old Marie as far as she's concerned.

I remain in the Castle this time for eight years. For the first six years I do nothing really to help myself. Though I manage to get my high school diploma, I accomplish little else that's positive. Often my energy is directed, still like a rebellious teenager, toward breaking the hospital rules; that always lands me in trouble. Too often I just avoid any kind of potentially helpful contact, drifting instead into my own troubled thoughts and feelings, eventually beginning a downhill slide that accelerates into an inescapable struggle with overpowering delusions and hallucinations.

I think part of the reason I do nothing is precisely because I'm so comfortable in the Castle. In a way different from all the other places in which I've lived, the Castle is my home, the staff and patients, my family. I've become a child who belongs there and with them. Though twenty-nine at the time of this latest admission, I have the maturity of a young teenager. My appearance hasn't changed since the earlier admissions—I'm still small and slight of build, weighing only one hundred and two pounds. The dungarees and shirts that I wear most of the time reinforce my image as a youngster. Staff treats me like a child; it's the easiest thing for them to do. And I want to be a child, to be taken care of, so I act like a child, sometimes intentionally.

Lying in bed that first night, I think of how good it is to be back. I'm safe. Now I can relax. The evening nurse tells me that Miss Wendall has become the head nurse on B-1. "We all really like that woman," she remarks. I remember Miss Wendall from my prior admissions. "She's certainly a good person," I recall fondly, "and very friendly to me." I try unsuccessfully to "puff up" my pillow, noticing that the hospital pillow is still as hard as it always was—"some things don't change," I laugh to myself. I picture Miss Wendall's face. A tall, extremely attractive woman, with smooth, olive-tinged skin, she always dresses in an immaculate white uniform with a lace hanky tucked in her breast pocket. Her starched white nurse's cap, with its black band, stands correctly in place on her neatly groomed, straight brown hair. Rolling over to go to sleep, I anticipate how happy I'll be to see Miss Wendall again in the morning, reassured she'll be there to take care of me.

"Rise and shine, ladies! Rise and shine, this ain't no vacation home!" The loud shouts of the nurses penetrate into my sleep and the bright ward lights flash on, making it hard to adjust my opening eyes to the room. Morning has come to the ward. I look around. Still sleepy women are getting up from their beds and dressing. I open my eyes wider, finally emerging from sleep, and continue to watch the scene.

"Marie, you slept really well last night. How do you feel?" One of the night nurses is talking to me as she's on her way out of the ward to go off her shift.

I don't respond. I remain in bed, waiting for someone to tell me to get up, but nothing is said. It's eerie. I keep waiting for someone or something, but I don't know who or what. And to make matters worse, a change has come over me since the night but I can't understand what it is. About thirty minutes later, a nurse shouts that it's smoking time. Smoking is now done in the sunporch. I grab a pack of cigarettes which I've hidden under my pillow and try to get up from my bed . . . but my body feels heavy, too heavy to move.

Several minutes pass. Finally, after a major effort, I'm able to rise from the bed. I place my feet solidly on the floor, and as I stand up, they feel like two pieces of lead. All I can do is shuffle slowly toward the sunporch. Something is terribly wrong and I want to tell that to one of the nurses, but I can't speak. Keeping my head down, I go over to a chair in the corner of the sunporch. When a nurse comes by to light my cigarette, I mumble a barely audible "thanks" and watch her walk over to a group of patients sitting at a table. Smoking my cigarette in silence, my head remaining slightly bowed, I can see the group of patients at the table. They're laughing and joking. I want to join in their fun but the thought of going over there frightens me. Instead, I finish my smoke and shuffle back to my bed. I'm relieved that I make it back. I lie down, pull the covers over my head and cry. This morning remains for a long time an aching memory.

Miss Wendall is one of the few forces that keeps pulling me toward life and hope. She's probably the most dedicated person I ever encounter at the Castle. Capable and self-assured, she's well respected by other staff who appreciate her genuine concern for patients. With her, everything always seems "in control." She's got a strong, serious personality which makes it hard to contradict her, but she really cares for us and isn't authoritarian. Miss Wendall comes on duty at seven in the morning, and, as she does every morning, carefully checks on each of the patients, writing down notes in their records. Now that she's finished her rounds and is sitting at her desk, I watch her. I'm too tired to go over to her, even to say hello . . . and I'm still too afraid to move about because my body feels heavy. But as I watch Miss Wendall, I feel better.

It takes a while before I realize how important Miss Wendall is to me. I'm deeply attached to her. She's the mother I never really had. Miss Wendall has faith in me, believing I'll get better long after others have given up on me. Others are fed up with my unwillingness to help myself, frustrated by my refusal to accept help from them, and driven to cynicism and despair by the increasing hopelessness of my situation. Miss Wendall loves me, even though I also put her through difficult times, stubbornly resisting her help, acting out to force her to discipline me. I trust her, and in my adolescent way, love her. Our relationship certainly has its ups and downs. But she's always there for me as no other person is and I let her care for me—and increasingly I rely on her support and encouragement.

Tranquilizers are just beginning to be used in the Castle, but I fight them, refusing to take them, struggling against their effects. Miss Wendall firmly believes in these new drugs and the antipsychotic drugs that have come into use. They're for her what they're intended to be—"wonder" drugs that can control mental illness. At different times Miss Wendall, usually with the assistance of several other nurses, has to force medication down my throat or into me with injections. But Miss Wendall gives the drugs to me with the conviction they'll make me better. One time, after a course of drugs is forced on me, I notice that the medication helps, calming me down. But as soon as I feel better, I start on a rampage, marching into the sunporch, throwing over all the chairs. Immediately, nurses are running into the porch and grab me. I fight back, kicking, punching, screaming out swears; but they're too many and too strong, and they shove me into the seclusion room. After a while, with me still screaming, they come into the room, and holding me down, give me a shot. Gradually, I drift off to sleep. The battle over medication is repeated many times— the outcome, being forced to take the drugs and usually spending some time in seclusion, is a foregone conclusion.

Eating is another battleground. Often I refuse to eat. I'm losing weight rapidly and in order to prevent my becoming debilitated, they force-feed me. One day Miss Wendall is trying to spoon feed me. Grimacing, I make it extremely hard for her to open my mouth. Then suddenly I've had enough. I push the spoon back at her, spilling the dark green pea soup over her clean white uniform. It looks disgusting and I turn away. I feel sick—I've just hurt the one person I can depend on. I've done it again . . . I'll be lost forever. Soon thereafter, Miss Wendall, along with three other attendants, forcibly leads me up a long flight of stairs and approaches the door to A-2. As we get closer to that back ward, my body goes limp and they have to drag me the rest of the way, into A-2 itself. I'm once again in the back ward of the Castle. I beg Miss Wendall to let me go back to B-1, grasping onto her uniform, blurting out my words with a sobbing voice. But it's useless. And so are my pleas in the subsequent days to the staff on A-2.

Miss Wendall feels I need A-2 because I've become uncontrollable. She's trying to help and at the same time believes I need some punishment or at least some disciplinary action. For me A-2 is only a punishment—and a punishment with its own unmatched cruelty. A-2 takes away my life. All I can breathe is the dead air of the lifeless patients, whose humanity has been almost totally robbed from them.

When I do leave A-2, I don't return to B-1; I'm taken to B-2 instead. B-2 is on a floor above B-1 and though it's not officially a back ward, it's certainly not as nice as B-1. There are more chronic patients there and many more restrictions. I remain on B-2 for approximately a year. At that point, Miss Wendall and the doctor in charge of the female patients determine that I'm a lot sicker than appears on the surface, and decide that I should return to B-1 where Miss Wendall can work more closely with me.

A change has come over me by the time I return to B-1. Not only am I unable to communicate, but my head feels hollow and inside of it a voice speaks out. It's a real voice that speaks loudly and sharply. It belongs to "Ma." Over and over again it says, "Marie, die! . . . Marie, die! . . . Marie die!" I spend most of my time sitting in a chair off the alcove listening to this voice, believing that Ma wants me to die but not knowing whether I should kill myself or whether I should defy Ma and keep on living. For hours at a time I'm immobilized with this terrible conflict, afraid to move, fearing any move will precipitate a decision.

At this time, a new woman doctor comes to the Castle. Dr. Baylor is a tall, older woman who's thoroughly dedicated to her work. Especially kind to patients, she's also respected by the staff. Though Dr. Baylor dresses conservatively, and her voice is firm, she's very friendly. The patients in the ward wait by the door for an hour or more for her arrival at morning rounds. When she comes she's barraged by patients, each asking for her attention and help—and she's always willing to listen. As she walks through the ward on her rounds, she's followed by a group of patients, still talking with her or just accompanying her. You never get from Dr. Baylor that punitive or rigid response which so many other staff show. As soon as she arrives, she takes an interest in me—that interest grows, becomes reciprocal, and begins to deepen into a real caring.

I still haven't told anyone that Ma's speaking to me but Miss Wendall suspects that I'm hearing something. Every once in a while, as I sit in the chair, my face tightens up, my lips mumble silent words, and my head shakes in protest.

Then I withdraw into myself, a blank stare masking the dialogue that continues to rage within.

Can't I tell someone about Ma's visits? I want support to resist her orders, and reassurance that I can disobey her. I don't want to kill myself, but I can't escape from that threat. Miss Wendall tries to reach out to me, but I'm afraid to tell her, afraid Ma will punish me. There's also another nurse, Mrs. Wolfson, whom I trust and wish to tell everything, but she's also unable to reach me. She makes many attempts to help but I continue to sit—entrapped by Ma's voice—from early morning until it's time to go to bed after supper. It's not until one day after Mrs. Wolfson stops working at the Castle that I approach Miss Wendall for the first time about Ma's commands.

"Miss Wendall . . . there's something wrong . . . real wrong. I'm hearing things and it's bad . . . bad things. Ma keeps telling me to die . . . she wants me to die. I don't want to die . . . but what can I do, she wants me to die. . . . And she doesn't leave me alone!"

It's very difficult to speak to Miss Wendall about Ma, and my words sometimes trail off into silence, as I avert my gaze. I'm frightened to tell her about Ma's voice because it shows that I'm sick and I'm afraid I won't get well.

Miss Wendall immediately sits me down at her desk so we can talk. Her words are soothing—I feel held and comforted. Then, she calls Dr. Baylor who orders a new medication for me. Having opened up enough to talk to Miss Wendall, I feel better. I'm just glad that she and Dr. Baylor know what's going on in my head. Ma's voice comes to me less frequently, and sometimes when it does, I sit with Miss Wendall, holding her hand. That helps. Eventually, Ma's voice will leave me.

Despite the fact that my life at the Castle is now chaotic and filled with anxiety most of the time, I never totally lose my ability to see myself and evaluate my condition—even if that vision is at times very weak and obscured. There are periods of lucidity when I realize how far things have deteriorated and how terrorized I become when Ma's voice speaks to me. This lucidity makes the situation even more painful as I can't really believe all this anxiety and "craziness" is happening to me.

But there's also relief from my suffering, and within the Castle, there are times of fun. I especially enjoy the companionship of the many patients now on B-1 who are age mates. We form a group, and while we can intensify each others' anxieties, we can also feed each others' healthy side by sharing good times. There are evenings when we sit by the old piano, as one of the patients plays songs and we all join in, singing at the top of our voices. During these moments I feel close to other people, and I'm happy because I'm part of the group, accepted by others.

There are other times when we relax, keeping each other company, enjoying a good laugh. It's really good therapy. These times keep me going when so much else is bringing me down, sapping my strength and hope.

Betty Morrison, a volunteer at the Castle, is also part of our group. It's great to see her coming onto the ward. She's always doing something to brighten our lives! She brings food—the kind we like, subs and stuff—and sometimes there's so much, she hauls it in on a wheelchair, or even on a stretcher! Betty's someone you can talk with. We become special friends and our talks become a really important part of my life. Being around Betty helps me feel normal. Every so often she invites some of us to visit at her house. One day a couple of us young female patients are over there, and her teenage son walks in—a really good-looking guy. Do we ever mature and become normal! He makes us grow up fast. Betty's there for me, pulling for me to get better, a companion even during the times when it seems I want nobody around.

I've also become friendly with Dr. Baylor now. She invites me to visit her home on the hospital grounds. Soon I'm a more regular guest, sometimes eating meals with her and her family, sometimes, when I'm feeling better, baby-sitting for her grandchildren. Babysitting is special—Dr. Baylor's confidence in me to do that means a lot. Dr. Baylor also arranges for me to clean her house periodically. All these times I spend at her place are important. It gets me out of the ward, away from its restrictions, and into a place that makes me feel needed and good—her house has nice soft furniture and plants in every window.

One day I'm asked to go down to clean Dr. Baylor's house—and to make matters even better, I can go with my friend Rose.

Rose and I are about the same age, in our early thirties. She's only five feet and, though quite stocky, has a very pretty face. We both could have been labeled "crazy"—and we are by the insensitive staff. But we're really just two good friends, suffering from the distress of mental illness, while still sharing our lives with each other, and enjoying each other's company in our home—the Castle.

We go to Dr. Baylor's house feeling relaxed and in a very playful mood. We're on a holiday! When we get there, we decide it would be a good idea to take the sheets off the bed and wash them. Dr. Baylor has one of those old-fashioned washing machines which is connected to a hose from the sink to fill it with water.

Now Rose isn't a hard worker. She's there at Dr. Baylor's house for some heavy "rest and relaxation." And rest she does. The soft chairs in Dr. Baylor's living room are irresistible. Flopped down in a big arm chair, she calls into the kitchen, "Marie, why don't you start the washer . . . and when it's ready we'll do the sheets. Me, I'm just gonna take it easy here."

I put the hose in the washer and turn it on.

"Marie, come in here," Rose calls out from the living room. "Come in and pull up a chair."

There's Rose, stretched out in the arm chair, smoking a cigarette, looking like a passenger on a million-dollar luxury cruise-liner. I join her in a cigarette and relax in another chair. We break into a full smile as we look at each other— and then we laugh . . . and laugh. We figure we have the whole day for ourselves, and we can eat when we want, smoke, do anything we please! We talk and talk, two special ladies enjoying the privilege of the elite rich.

A realization suddenly disturbs me! "Dr. Baylor comes home for lunch at noon," I say to Rose, "and she's prompt!" I look at my watch—quarter to twelve. We go towards the kitchen so we'll look busy when Dr. Baylor arrives.

The sound is strange, like a little mountain stream. At first it doesn't mean anything. Then I wonder . . . and then I become alarmed. Nearly slipping, I splash through the water which now covers the kitchen floor. Finally I reach the washer and frantically turn off the faucet where the hose is attached, while the remaining water spills over the side of the washer. Alarm turns to laughter as I survey the kitchen under water. Then I return to the business at hand.

"Rose, our plans have changed," I announce, barely able to stop laughing. "It's work time." And for the next fifteen minutes, racing against the clock, we mop up the water. The last mop full is wrung out and the floor dried one minute before noon. Dr. Baylor arrives promptly at twelve.

"Now that's what I call a clean kitchen!" she states with pride, feeling good about the quality of our work. "That's wonderful. But you really didn't have to wash the floor!"

Rose and I look at each other, but our laughter remains within. We're just good little patients and we thank Dr. Baylor for her compliment.

"That's the last time I go out to work with you," Rose says in mock seriousness as we walk back to the ward. "Do you really think I'm meant to work? Work can make you tired, you know!"

10. *"I'm Really Crazy Now"*

I have my ups and downs on B-1. During one of my better periods, I'm transferred to C-1, an open ward where patients are allowed to go out on the hospital grounds unsupervised. With only one nurse in charge of the open ward, I feel lots of pressure to be in control of my behavior if I want to stay there. It's on the open ward that I begin a significant change for the worse—I regress to become Pat, the five-year-old I was before being adopted by Ma and Pa.

I don't like being Pat. She's only a little five-year-old, can't get around so well and is so easily frightened. But I've become Pat—spinning out of control, I've ended up in her little body. I walk slowly, painfully slowly, and totally terrified into Dr. Baylor's office. I'm just a little girl. Who's going to take care of me?

"Marie . . . Marie . . . are you all right?" Dr. Baylor is so worried about me—I've never seen her face look so worried. She's just read the note I wrote on her pad: "I'm not Marie, I'm Pat."

Now Dr. Baylor looks at me intently and begins asking a series of simple questions I find too difficult to answer.

"Marie, I'm taking you back to B-1. It'll be better for you there."

I don't resist. Whatever Dr. Baylor says is all right with me. I don't have enough strength to argue with anyone. As she takes me back to B-1, I'm a little girl being led home.

But it isn't that I'm just Pat. I'm both Pat and the person who knows that being Pat is itself a sign of my sickness. I never totally lose sight of that difference, though the degree to which I'm aware I've regressed varies, and there are times when I don't know a life outside of Pat's child world.

Dr. Baylor feels the closed ward environment of B-1 is necessary given my regression into childhood. She also puts me back on a medication program. And to emphasize the seriousness of my condition, she assigns me the first bed next to the nurses' station so that I can be closely observed. As I lie there, I feel myself going further back into time—I become an infant. I roll to my side with my body curled up into a ball and pull my head down toward my stomach. Then, I start to whine. The sound of my voice frightens me. It's the wail of a new-born infant. I stick my thumb into my mouth and begin rocking my body back and forth, finding the motion soothing.

"Who's going to stop that awful whining?" one of the nurses complains. "This ain't no nursery!"

Though I appear unaware of my surroundings, I hear her words. They're cruel and hurt me deeply. My anger rises. I know the state I'm in, but I also know that I didn't bring it on myself and I can't get out of it. I'm glad when the evening nurse comes on duty. I've come to trust her and feel safer with her around. She orders some medication for me and for a little while I'm calmer.

I remain on the bed until the medication has worn off and then get up to go into the sunporch. I walk over to a chair and sit down. The room looks strange, as though I'm watching a movie but am not really part of it. Then, an invisible force engulfs me and I feel a force raise my arms in the air. This force is controlling my motions—I make no effort to fight it. It seizes my arms and moves them wildly in various directions. When my arms finally come to rest on the chair, I look at my hands. My fingers have become flesh-covered snakes! "You're really crazy now," I whisper to myself and start to sob, between deep panicky breaths. I go back to my bed, a hopeless and miserable wreck.

Whenever I become Pat, I get very scared. Also, when I'm Pat, my head doesn't feel right. A tight band seems to be strapped around my skull, giving me dull headaches and a whoozy feeling whenever I walk. Though my experiences of being the five-year-old Pat subside, my illness begins taking other, even more frightening forms. And though some awareness of my general situation as a patient in the hospital keeps reappearing, I continue to suffer delusions and hallucinations. I'm no longer in control of my life but, rather, controlled by forces beyond my real world.

The nights are full of terror for the ward is no longer a place where I can sleep undisturbed. The darkness is shattered by the night dimmers which cast shadows that move across the entire room, covering the walls and the ceiling. I'm lying in a misty swamp overgrown with eerie weeping willows. Screaming for help, I run the full length of the ward with monsters in pursuit. The faces of the nurses are no longer kind and motherly. They become grotesque masks painted in rosy piercing colors. The nurses become devils who have invaded the earth. I'm in Hell. Only thirty-two and already in Hell.

Often I'm petrified. I just think I'm going to die. There are these beds in the ward, all in a row, and as I look at them, I believe that the patients lying on them are dead. I don't know why I believe that or how it happens, but I see them as dead bodies. And the bed to which I'm assigned is the first one in this long row. It's empty now, but I know that if I lie down on it, I too will be dead. I'm supposed to sleep on that bed, but all I can think is: "I don't want to die." I'm afraid to lie down on my bed because I'm afraid of dying.

I'm paralyzed with conflict—I'm tired, so tired, and I want to rest, but I can't go near my bed. I go up to the nurse, to plead for help, but I can hardly utter a word, as I'm retreating more and more into silence with my deepening illness.

"That bed . . . that bed is for dead people." The words barely leave my mouth, and I'm sure the nurse doesn't hear them. She doesn't acknowledge my desperate reach for survival.

"What are you standing there for?" she shouts, her voice almost knocking me over. "Go back to bed. Go back to your bed."

I try to follow her order, but can't move. I turn to her and all I can say is, "I'm scared . . . the people in those beds are dead, you know . . . I can't go to bed." I'm reduced to a whimper.

The nurse's response is sharp and unyielding. "Listen," she insists, "if you want to be crazy, then you be crazy on someone else's shift. Don't be crazy on mine. You get into the bed."

I have no choice. I go over to the bed and slowly lie down. But all night I keep looking at the beds around me, wondering if I'm still breathing.

I survive that night, but the fear of dying stays with me for many nights. And the penetrating knowledge that I'm now living in Hell becomes inescapable.

Several days later Florence comes to visit. She is an intelligent woman in her mid-thirties. She and I became friends when we were both downstairs on the open ward. After I was transferred back to the closed ward of B-1, she remained on the open ward. Florence is in the hospital because she killed her two children in order to "save them from their suffering." She also talks a lot about wanting to die so that she can go to Heaven. On the open ward, we would spend hours talking, while sitting in chairs on the porch or while walking around the hospital. We feed each other's minds and hearts.

Now I'm lying in my bed, still captured by the newly formed fear of dying, not moving, hoping death will pass me by. Suddenly Florence appears over me.

"I've come to visit you, Marie," she says. "I heard you weren't feeling too well."

Here I am, feeling very sick, thinking I'm not going to make it, terrified of others as well as myself. And here is Florence, coming to visit me.

"How are you feeling, Marie?" Florence continues, "I heard they sent you up to this closed ward. You sure don't look too good. Is there anything I can do to help?"

My mind races, but clearly. "Gee, Florence, I don't think so. I'm really feeling okay. Thanks anyways, but I'm doing all right."

"Are you sure?"

"Yeah, Florence, I feel fine. Nothing's wrong . . . I'm a little depressed but, y'know, that'll be okay."

"Well, if you ever need me, if you ever need my help, just let me know."

"I'll do that," I assure her, "and thanks, thanks for coming by."

"I'll come back tomorrow to see you again."

"Aw gee, Florence, I don't like to bother you . . . "

From some deep place within my crushing pain and anxiety, a lightness emerges, allowing me to see the crazy humor of my situation, and that gives me breathing space. I never have the heart to tell Florence that her dream of going to heaven has ended. "Florence," I say to myself, "you think you're going to die and go to Heaven. I hate to tell you but you're already dead and you're in Hell. This here ward is Hell. You've died, Florence, just like the rest of us here, but you just don't know it." I almost laugh to myself when I realize Florence can stop worrying about dying now!

I'm kept in bed for most of the two years I remain in B-1. The staff believes I'm too sick to move about. I retreat into my bed, pulling the covers over my head, usually curling up in a fetal position, barely moving, terrified that any movement will release some frightening voices or sounds.

Miss Wendall and some of the other friendly nurses try to keep me in bed because they wish to give me rest and comfort. But sometimes I feel a burning sensation creep over my body. It's not painful, but it prevents me from sleeping. Other times, nurses who are less than friendly use my bed as a punishment, ordering me to stay there or ridiculing my general fear of moving. They shame and scare me into staying put, making me more afraid I can't move, or will fall or be pursued by monsters if I do.

Though I stay in bed most of the time, periodically I venture into the ward or to the lounge. At times I want to go to the lounge because that's where the TV is and also where the patients go to socialize. The ward just has beds. But getting to the lounge is torture.

As I approach the lounge, the floor begins to tilt upwards, the angle becoming more radical as I get closer.

The windows which line the wall across from the entrance drop lower toward the floor, and become opaque and confusing as if water is covering them. I struggle up the floor, barely able to keep my balance, the floor shifting and moving unexpectedly beneath me. I have to stand on the balls of my feet in order to keep from falling. Lurching from one piece of furniture in the lounge to the next, grasping onto each succeeding piece, I inch my way toward my favorite chair. When I finally come to within touching distance of that chair, I desperately fall forward toward it, the floor sending my body into one final dizzying trip, and I sink with relief into its cushions. Exhausted, but somewhat relaxed, I light up a cigarette and spend a bit of time smoking and looking at the TV or at other patients. I don't really watch anything or understand fully what I see, but the images which pass before me give some enjoyment.

Then, when I begin to get anxious about being in the lounge, I realize I have to start the terrifying journey back to my bed. As my anxiety in staying in the chair becomes unbearable, I set out back through that awful territory, with the tilting floor testing the depth of my will. At the other end I emerge to the relative peace of my bed. But inevitably, in the vicious cycle I'm caught in, I'm compelled to leave the bed again and run the gauntlet to the lounge.

Sometimes, when friendly nurses are on duty and I'm feeling relatively better, the lounge becomes a more attractive place. Then I journey to the lounge, through the still fearsome tilting floors, more because I want to see TV or see people or smoke, rather than because I feel driven from my bed. Those friendly nurses, and especially Miss Wendall, encourage me to get out of bed. "You'll feel better, Marie," they say. "You'll feel stronger if you can walk around a bit." I don't know where my wish to respond to their help comes from, but it's deeply buried, emerging only occasionally.

I never really understand why I walk on the balls of my feet when I try to negotiate the sliding morass of that lounge floor. All I know is that I usually don't feel the floors, and walking on the balls of my feet gives me more leverage and support.

There are other times when I feel driven from my bed and begin racing down the ward, screaming. The nurses chase after me, trying to grab me. I want to run through a window to escape from my fear. Racing down the ward screaming, I'm struggling to stay alive. If I can just get that extra bit of energy to run faster and farther, then I won't die. Running beyond what I believe is possible helps me run beyond my fear. And sometimes I'm running away from my bed, which becomes a place where I'm fighting to stay alive. I scream as loud as I can, noises and sounds, not words. Only by screaming can I breathe enough to stay alive—screaming is my desperate last-ditch breathing.

When I have to race down the hall, I'll usually run on the balls of my feet, with my arms extended stiffly into the air. Being on the balls of my feet is the only way I can be— I have no choice. It's the way I've worked it out so I can remain upright—the only way! And I have no choice about my arms either. There's a force pulling them up and I can't resist. Running, running faster and faster, until I'm racing.

"There goes Marie, the Castle's own space cadet. Off on another journey down the runway. Up, up, and away . . . the space-shot's off!" The playful teasing of the nurses fills my ears.

As I race down the hall, I hear their words. "Don't they realize what's happening to me?" I think. "Don't they realize

I don't want to run on the balls of my feet, I don't want to keep my hands up . . . but I have to, I've no choice. They don't even know how painful it is for to me to do these things. It's so hard to keep on my toes and keep my hands up . . . it's so hard."

I'm not angry at their teasing because their attitude is often friendly and playful. They help lighten the burden I feel on those runs. I even laugh with them sometimes. I appreciate then how funny it must seem with me on my toes running down the ward. But the nurses don't understand the other side—what I'm feeling *inside*. They don't know how miserable I am as a space-cadet, how hard it is to have the force pull my hands up, how frightened I am that I might become a space-cadet forever. Why can't they understand that I've no choice? How could they know that for me, moving in any way, as a space-cadet or not, is better than lying in bed and not moving at all? And the faster I move the better, because I believe that as my body moves and moves faster, I'm getting away from being slow and sick—two states which are connected in my mind. The nurses know none of these things because I don't tell them. I'm barely talking with anyone about anything.

Time means nothing to me. I don't know how much time has passed, and weeks pass into months without my knowledge. I become afraid of everything. Though a particular terrifying experience might be brief, the fear it generates invades my whole existence, lingering on. I smell funeral flowers throughout the ward and as I near the kitchen, a smell of gas suffocates me. I become one with the monsters who dominate my world. When I look in the mirror, I sometimes see only the face of an evil devil-like creature. I can't comb my hair because it's become like strands of wire, and my lips are no longer human, but puffed-up, rosy hunks of flesh. Unexpectedly, I become an ice-monster. My body starts to freeze up and soon turns into ice. Shivering uncontrollably, my two eyeteeth form into daggers of dripping ice-fangs. The cold numbs me and then I feel nothing, not my body, not my self. I've scared myself into icy oblivion.

Though I rarely acknowledge it, my life depends on the support I get during these awful two years. The staff wants someone to be with me as much as possible; they feel I need that kind of care, even protection. Several times I've tried to take my life. Once I crashed through a window, hoping the glass would cut into me and I could bleed to death. Yes . . . I need protection.

Some of my friends among the patients come up to my bed every so often, maybe offer me a cigarette and sit with me so I can smoke it there. And they stay on a while, just sitting, keeping me company. I don't really talk much— sometimes not at all—but they sit there anyway. I know they're there, and feel really good about their visit, and I guess that comes through because they keep coming. Part of me wishes I could talk more with them, but I'm cut off and isolated, unable to break through a wall that's around me. Sometimes one of the nurses comes by with a sub, asking if I want it. I might nod my head, and she leaves it for me in the nurses' refrigerator, with my name on it. Later in the night I might go to the refrigerator and eat part of that sub, though it's always hard to swallow any kind of food.

During one period, staff puts me and my friend Rose together in our own sleeping room. Maybe they think Rose can help me. Well, at times it seems to work. She's always talking to me and sometimes makes me want to laugh—if only I could. One day I'm feeling a little better.

I'm still seeing and hearing things, but for some reason, they're not as scary today. Rose is talking on and on, commenting about patients on the ward, complaining about the food and the lack of cigarettes. Then her tone changes—she becomes a little more serious. "Gee, Marie, y'know, you seem to be having a real hard time."

Rose's right. I like talking with her and I'm glad she understands the state I'm in. I don't hesitate to tell her about my frightening feelings because we talk about everything.

"You know, Rose," I respond, feeling freer now to talk than I have in a long time, "it sometimes gets really bad. I get into some of the rooms here in the hospital and I can smell funeral flowers. I can smell them all over the place."

"Is that right?" Rose says, showing real interest. "You really smell them?"

"Yeah, that's what I smell."

"Y'know what?" she asks, in a little bit of a whisper. "You know what I smell?"

"No."

"Cow manure."

I can't believe she says that. "Come on, Rose, you gotta be kidding."

"No," she continues, "I smell cow manure."

"You know, Rose, I know you drink. I mean everybody knows you're in here for drinking. Do you think the booze kinda went to your head? Are you trying to put me on?"

"I wouldn't put you on," she affirms. "I really smell that manure."

"Can you smell it now?"

"Yeah, I can smell it right now!"

"Rose, I can smell the funeral flowers, but what you say doesn't make sense to me."

"And you know something else, Rose," I add, "I also feel like there's a wind coming over me sometimes. All at once this wind blows over me and chills me."

Unexpectedly the window in the room flies open, and a wind fills the room, shooting out the door.

"There it comes," shouts Rose, as she runs out of the room, straight for the nurses' desk. I begin to laugh, though the laughter must break through layers of pained silence. There is Rose trying to explain to the nurse on duty how powerful my fantasy has become, how the wind I'm imagining has nearly blown her over.

"Rose, you go back down to your room or I'll have to separate you from Marie," the nurse admonishes, an outsider to the fun that lay within even the most apparently frightening of experiences.

During the night, in our room, I look at Rose to see if she's having any trouble with the wind, laughing to myself, then laughing with her as I say, "I don't know, but there goes that breeze again."

We actually smell these things—though I can't believe Rose smells the manure, and she can't believe I smell the funeral flowers. But we listen to each other's story of what occupies, captures, even tortures our minds. We listen, and hear, and that helps each of us. Respecting our differing hallucinations, we respect each other as people. The symptoms of our emotional problems are also opportunities for comradeship and laughter. To the outsider, we're two "crazy" kids, but we're also two friends teasing each other, having fun. I smell gas too. I don't tell Rose that.

More usually, each day brings its own horror and I'm constantly yelling and screaming in fear, struggling to keep horrors away—but they keep coming. One night, I'm crouched up on a bed, in one of the private rooms off the central ward, both exhausted and terrified. I'm waiting for death—I can't survive one more horror. Mrs. Williams, an evening nurse, looks into the room, and finding me there, takes hold of my arm and leads me to the seclusion room. Begging her not to leave me there, I cling desperately to her skirt. She eases down to the mattress and sits with me for the rest of the night. When daylight comes into the seclusion room window, my body relaxes. With Mrs. Williams's help I've survived. I'm still alive.

Through most of this two year period on B-1, when I'm at my sickest, beset by fears all around me, I'm on a controversial drug program. At the recommendation of Dr. Baylor and Miss Wendall, I'm given massive dosages of Stellazine, which at the time is a new antipsychotic medication. The maximum daily dosage recommended is 40 milligrams, but by the end of the program, I'm receiving 2,500 milligrams a day. Miss Wendall and Dr. Baylor are trying to help. They've read about an experiment that suggests massive dosages of Stellazine given to schizophrenics can get them to regress. Eventually a breaking point is reached where the drug effects act like a shock, and the patients are led to insights which will reduce their psychosis. Since I now have the diagnosis of schizophrenia, and since my condition seems to be deteriorating, Miss Wendall and Dr. Baylor institute the massive dosage program as a last resort, trying desperately to break into my tortured world and pull me out.

Other staff violently disagree with that drug program because of what they see—as the program progresses I'm getting sicker, both psychologically and physically. My hallucinations and delusions are increasing as my physical health deteriorates, with severe weight loss and fatigue.

They can't stand to see me stay on the regime and they transfer out of the ward rather than administer the drugs to me. I don't realize this is happening—all I know is some of my friends on the staff don't come by anymore and I figure they no longer like me. I have to take fistfuls of pills each day, or receive two shots in my buttocks. My buttocks become like leather from the shots, and the nurses have to jab the needles in with all their strength. They use the needles when I'm panicky, or sometimes just because they want a quicker effect. After a while, my resistance to the regime weakens. I won't say I comply, but I no longer have the will or energy to resist.

I'm in a vicious cycle with that drug program. When I experience something terrifying, they increase my dosage as a way to counteract that terror. But the dosage itself makes me more terrified, and that leads to yet another increase.

I'll never forget how these drugs feel—I die from them. When they give me the medications, I start feeling very, very weak, and very, very scared . . . and then I start screaming, screaming to try to get some energy so I won't die. I'm dying and if I don't force myself to scream, that's the end. I have no breath left, I'm choking, and if I can just scream, I can breathe . . . I won't drown . . . I won't go under. And then I can't even breathe enough to scream, and I can't breathe at all . . . and I die . . . struggling, I die. This happens each time I'm given the drugs. When I come to, I find myself being restrained by several nurses and being really sick, throwing up continually. There's a basin filled with vomit and I know I've been throwing up before I've come to. I'm not sure whether I'm glad to be alive—I feel too sick.

Eventually, Miss Wendall and Dr. Baylor can't continue with the program any longer. They've suffered through my worsening condition only because they're convinced the massive dosages might work. It's a desperate choice, but now my condition has deteriorated so badly that their conviction withers. I'm down to eighty-seven pounds, have lost most of my teeth, and am in a state of almost constant terror. One night I almost die from the damage the drugs are doing to my liver. I'm rushed to the medical building and, with emergency procedures, saved. The faces of the doctors who are working on me become so grotesque that I forget even my physical pain. The next day, the drug program is stopped.

To this day, I don't know exactly how much of my sickness during that experimental massive-dosage program, including all the horrible monsters and distortions, was drug-induced. But in light of what I've learned recently from several professional psychiatric evaluations, I believe that in addition to the illness I was already suffering from then, the panic disorder, I was also suffering from a toxic reaction to overmedication or what is called today "toxic psychosis." The medication made my panic attacks worse. In addition to being overmedicated, I was wrongly medicated—my diagnosis of schizophrenia turns out to be a misdiagnosis. From recent psychiatric consultation I've learned that my diagnosis should have been endogenous depression and panic attack.

But even after the massive dosages of Stellazine stop, I don't get better. I rarely eat and don't put on any weight, though Miss Wendall leaves instructions with the nursing staff to be sure I'm fed whenever possible. But some of the more insensitive nurses ignore her orders. "If you want any food, you'll just have to get out of bed and get it yourself like the rest of the people here!" one of the nurses sneers. But doesn't she know that I'm not allowed off my bed according to Miss Wendall's instructions? And right now there's no strength to leave my bed even if I'm allowed to. When those insensitive nurses are on duty, I just lie on my bed and pull the covers over me, pretending to be asleep. My body, though weakened, still carries to my mind the devastating effects of the horrors that have become my life. There's nowhere to turn, nowhere even to move, certainly no escape. I've been in agony almost every day, for nearly two years.

11. *Fighting For My Life*

"*My* bones . . . they just stick out," I observe in disbelief. Standing in front of a mirror, I'm looking at this person whose sallow flesh drapes over bony protuburances, like a wet cloth hung out to dry over a leafless, scraggly bush. This is one of my better days. Usually I'm confined to bed, and the nurses feed and bathe me there. Today I've walked, slowly and still on the balls of my feet, to the bathroom, and am about to step into the shower when I pass by the mirror.

My debilitated naked body shocks me. It shows the ravages of my illness and severe weight loss—I'm still weighing only eighty-six pounds. "I'm really sick," I moan. "Now I'm really sick." That realization comes to me more and more recently, surrounded as I've been by a hostile environment of garish and searing colors, with grostesque faces hovering over my bed or passing by me in the ward. I'm petrified that my sickness will become permanent, that I'll have to walk on the balls of my feet for the rest of my life, tormented by the devilish presence of others.

The next day lying in my bed, as usual, I hide my face under the covers so that I don't have to see anyone, so I don't have to see the monsters which the nurses and other patients always become. For some reason, I sit up. Miss Wendall's coming down the hall. Her face melts into a horrible expression, sneering at me with large, crooked, dirty fangs. I can't bear it!

A new realization comes to me. "This horror that I'm in . . . that's the world Miss Wendall and those other nurses talk about . . . that's the crazy world . . . I'm in the crazy world now. I'm one of those patients they're always talking about!" I get really scared—"I'm crazy." But I'm also amazed—something in me clicks in a new way. "Those nurses talk about crazy people being in another world," I continue, talking to myself, "and this is what I've come to. I'm in that 'other world.' " My mind's racing, and I fight panic. One more thought comes to me, "I don't like this world I'm in. I don't want to be here!"

I have to go back under the covers; things are happening too fast and I'm getting too scared again. But something is different. When I sit up again, I look at the room. It has become a cold, piercing shade of red. "I don't like this room," I cry to myself, "but I don't know how to get out of here. People think we die and go to Hell. But this is Hell. This is Hell and they don't even know it. I've got to get out of here!" Panic returns; I try to gain some control of myself. "But can I get out?" my thoughts almost burst into words. "Dear God," I'm now praying, "Dear God, I don't know if I can get out."

Then some thoughts come to me more clearly than any have in the last two years of my nightmarish existence on B-1. I'm engulfed in the horrors of that "other world" the nurses say crazy people live in. And I'm struggling to find a way out. I remember what the nurses always advise: "If you do some physical work, you'll get better." I start talking to myself with a resolve that's stronger than anything I've been able to muster in many, many years: "If the real world where the nurses live is out there . . . and this is the crazy, unreal world that I'm in . . . well, maybe if I can just touch the real world, maybe I can come back to it." Right away I doubt my idea, warning myself, "I don't know if it's going to work." I'm frightened again—I'll fail, and sink forever back into that "other world."

Clarity and resolve return. "What am I going to do?" I ask myself, and the answer comes quickly: "I'm sicker than I've ever felt before . . . I just can't go on this way anymore. There's no choice. I've got to get better . . . or I'll die. I've got to fight . . . to try. This touching is the only thing I know how to do." And as I lie in bed, I make a little plan. "Maybe if I touch something physical, real things will come back . . . maybe if I work with my hands, I can get back to the real world."

That night, before I go to sleep, the thoughts of the day return: "That's what I'm going to do. I'm going to touch things and see if I can come back to the real world." As I keep repeating the plan to myself, a resolve is deepening— it's a new feeling, which I can't fully accept as my own. But then I warn myself again, "Marie, you've got no choice. Otherwise you'll be permanently crazy. It's now or never!"

This plan will take every bit of my energy because my hands are still not under my control. I can't feel anything with them and when I look at them, they don't belong to me. "How can I touch things without any hands?" Now I'm scared again. "I'll try," is my only response. I sleep through the night without screaming—a rare event.

Miss Wendall is on duty in the morning. She allows me to walk about when I want to. Most of the other nurses insist I stay on my bed because they're afraid I'll fall if I get up. I'm still walking only on the balls of my feet and appear unsteady to them. But I walk this way because of the invisible force taking me along, and I hold onto the walls just enough to let the force do its work. They don't understand that.

Seeing Miss Wendall supports me. I remember the thoughts of the night. I get up from my bed and go into the little dormitory off the ward where some old patients sleep. They're out eating breakfast, and an attendant is in the dorm making up their beds.

Walking over to one of the beds, I reach out to the mattress. I look at the hands that come out from my body—they're hairy and unfamiliar. I can't feel the fingers which stick out from the ends—they're like sleeping snakes. My plan . . . I remember it and feel a surge of strength to try. Something in me tries to connect with those fingers. They move awkwardly, shedding their snake-like appearance. They hurt, and it takes all my energy to break through the stiffness in which they're locked. I reach for the bed covers and have to hold on to the bed for balance. I'm really glad! "My fingers, they're holding me up! They're working for me." I begin to move my fingers over the sheets and blankets, in a feeble attempt to make up one of the beds.

I don't get very far, but I try and for me, it's far enough. It's the very first thing I attempt to do in my new plan.

This change doesn't occur only because of the insights from the previous two days, for even during the times when I was terribly sick, a part of me dimly saw my condition and fought for my survival, ever so weakly. Running down the hall, I may have been just a screaming "space-cadet" to others, but that was my way of fighting against the slowness and stillness of lying in bed, which for me meant a worsening of my sickness and death itself. And my screams were at times gasps for the air of life, a frantic attempt to breathe and be alive.

During these terrible times, members of the staff reached out to help, but I made no obvious progress. Some of those who tried to help gave up, and that frightened me, because I didn't want to be left alone in a hopeless existence. But others stayed with me, at times sitting with me on my bed, or holding me, keeping me company as I journeyed through some terrible event—since I didn't talk much, that's all they could do.

But especially during these past two days, and to some extent for several weeks, I realize that I'm suffering more than I ever thought was possible—and I just can't take any more. The night my plan emerges I know that it's up to me whether or not I succumb totally to the illness that's destroying me. I don't instantaneously develop a full sense of responsibility, but I do turn the corner. I don't know exactly what I'll do, but I'm more ready to fight for my life than just fight against the monsters who try to kill me.

This resolve isn't new, though its intensity is. I've always wanted to be treated with respect. When the staff treated me as a nonperson, dragging me off to seclusion like an animal to be punished, or forcing me into shock treatment like a piece of flesh to be operated on, or what was more painful, ignoring or ridiculing my anguish and terror-driven behaviors, some part of me fought back.

When I was still an adolescent, staff thought I was just a fresh young kid. That was true in part. But I was also fighting for my life and demanding their respect for me as a person. As I grew older in the hospital, I wasn't as much the rebellious teenager, but still I fought. When the drugs threatened to take away my dignity as a person, I tried to battle them as long as I could. I wanted a choice in my treatment, to say "no" to something that was so painful. I couldn't fight back all the time—for periods of time I was too weak or frightened to do anything but comply, or too confused even to know what was happening to me. I've always fought—but gave up too easily and too soon.

Though I never *totally* lost hope for any long period of time, I often felt hopeless. But now reality hits me. I'm so sick that I could become permanently hopeless—unless I do something about it. I'm shocked into some action to get better.

I turn a corner; seeing myself at the bottom of the pit, I resolve to climb out. But the climb isn't easy, nor is it smooth. I have to crawl out of that pit, and there are continual setbacks. It's slow, painfully slow work, testing my determination with every movement toward health— and my determination grows as a result.

To this day I don't know why the insights of those two days came when they did or how I began to translate them into action.

Faces of people still become monstrous, the floor still tilts up, forcing me to struggle for balance, and fear remains in every corner, leaping out to suffocate me. I try to ignore these terrors of my daily existence, hoping they'll leave me alone as my contact with the real world increases. Yet they don't *just* leave. They linger on, only gradually decreasing their attacks on me. But something else is growing, something which at times had nearly vanished for good—hope. Hope that I can get better, hope for my life, hope that I can make it to the outside world. Hope feeds my resolve and is fed in return by the growing resolve. I'm developing strength to meet the terrors which invade my life. I'm not hiding under the covers as much.

Starting simply and carefully, I try to bring in life by touching things, just touching things to remove the dead numbness from my body. Then I attempt work tasks, as a therapy. I try different activities. It takes strength and courage to try—I always worry that I'll fail—but doing the activity gives me strength and courage to try something more. Sitting on my bed, I start to play with a deck of cards from the nurses' desk. I pick up one card at a time, trying to feel my fingers through touching the cards. I move a group of cards from hand to hand, trying to shuffle them. They fall to the bed, but I pick them up again. It seems like hours go by with my trying, more or less successfully, to shuffle the cards. My fingers finally begin to feel the shiny surface of the cards, and their sharp edges, and finger coordination starts to return. That's what I'm seeking. It's good to feel even a little coordinated!

My next goal is to eat without help. I go to the kitchen, walking toward the refrigerator. Even though I want to open it, I have to lean against it at first because the floor throws me off balance. But eventually I open the refrigerator and, with great concentration, pour myself a glass of milk. Good, only a little bit spills. The milk tastes awful, but I force myself to drink it. Drinking that one glass is so hard! As time goes on, I eat other foods and eat more regularly, though for a long while all food still repels me and I gag on it, wishing to vomit. I just shove the food down, like a punishment. "But I gotta eat," I say to myself. "That's part of getting well."

I go back each day to the old ladies' dorm, and soon I'm able to make up a bed, even though I have to keep holding on to the bed with one hand for balance. "If I can make up one bed today," I affirm to myself, "I'll do all right." When I reach the point where I can make several beds, I change the activity. In the kitchen, I lug around one of those big, heavy mops, cleaning up the kitchen floor.

Nobody on the staff really knows what I'm doing. They see me trying different activities, and most just watch. A few support my efforts to complete the tasks. But no one knows that each activity is part of my plan to touch the real world, to work . . . to get better. And that's how I want it—I want to do it myself. Sure, the support of others is very important, but right now I really want to get better on my own efforts.

One day, resting on my bed, observing the nurses going about their daily tasks as I usually do, I see something new—the nurses are ordinary people. Though they're caring for me and the other patients, the focus of their "real" lives is outside. At the end of their shift, they have a home and family to go to. It's a painful realization—the nurses work at the Castle to help achieve their personal goals on the outside, and they're going to continue on their own way in that real world, *bypassing* me completely. I want to go into the outside world too and establish my own place there. The thought scares me. "I'm still sick," I protest, looking to myself for some respite. Instead I resolve to take the next step.

After having been on B-1 for two years, I feel ready to leave. After the excruciating terror of nearly two years, the last three months, during which I've put my plan for recovery into action, has been a good period for me. Also, my new medication program seems to calm me down. I feel more confident, as the intense horrors associated with the earlier massive dosage program have vanished. Though I'm still hampered by invisible forces and compelled to walk unsteadily on the balls of my feet, the garish, frightening colors appear only occasionally, and the faces of the staff are almost always normal.

I want to take a first step out of B-1 by venturing outdoors, to the hospital grounds. To do this I have to get permission from Dr. Baylor. Even though my condition has been improving over the last three months, I still don't talk very much. Approaching Dr. Baylor will be difficult. Miss Wendall, who usually intercedes with Dr. Baylor on my behalf, has transferred to the night shift, so I don't have her to speak for me. And the staff worries me. Most are invested in patients staying helpless so they can be more easily managed and manipulated. Maybe they'll ridicule my desire to go outdoors, and maybe some will even undercut my efforts to get better. "It would be better to keep my plan secret," I reflect, "and let them keep wondering what I'm up to."

When Dr. Baylor comes on the ward one afternoon, I walk up to her. "Hi, Dr. Baylor . . . could I . . . I want to talk with you!" My words, though not very loud, catch her by surprise—and me too! Her smile shows she's pleased I'm talking. As she leads me into a small conference room off the ward, she turns warmly to me, "It's good to hear you talk, Marie. Let's sit in here and you can tell me how you've been."

"Dr. Baylor, I need to get better, and I have to . . . I'm working on it." I begin speaking even before we sit down. Then I detail some of the activities I've done and my successes, and describe my treatment plan. "I want to get out," I keep repeating. Then I propose my request: to have access to the hospital grounds, eventually working my way to C-1, the open ward. "I've done all I can on B-1 to help myself, now . . . it's the next step now . . . I need to move on." Even though I can hear my voice speaking, the firmness of tone is very unfamiliar. Probably Dr. Baylor won't grant me permission to go outdoors, especially since I remain very unsteady, walking on the balls of my feet. And I begin to worry that I shouldn't have told her about my treatment plan. It's worked so well so far, and it's been my secret.

She agrees! I can't describe my joy! Now I can continue my treatment program and continue to work with Dr. Baylor. Her friendship and faith in me have always been so important; now she's part of my new treatment plan.

Dr. Baylor asks to be kept informed of what I'm doing and how I feel. "And I may give you some advice along the way," she adds with a smile. "And I'll continue your medication . . . but is there anything else that I can do right now to help with your plan?"

I appreciate her question—it's sincere and kind. But I am convinced that I have to develop my own plan and put it into practice.

"Stand by me . . . that's what I need. Could you give me permission to do the things I ask for when I ask you?" I know that's all I need.

Dr. Baylor gives me her assurance, "I'll try . . . I'll try to do that as best I can."

After Dr. Baylor leaves the ward, I stay another hour. Then I take my first steps on the way outside to the hospital grounds. Once again I'm terrified, but now not because of piercing colors or faces, but because of fear of failure. I walk toward the main door, holding on to the walls because I'm very unsteady. Everyone seems to be looking at me, waiting for me to fail. The main door is so heavy—it takes all my effort to open it. And the stairs to the grounds are steep and partially covered with the snow of winter. As I look down them, I become dizzy, and my descent becomes torturously awkward, each step taking time and demanding effort.

Finally on the grounds, I go off the path, onto the snow-covered lawn. I reach down. The snow is soft . . . inviting. Picking up a little, I bring it close to my face. It's clean and good. Reaching down again . . . and again . . . and again, I let the snow fly in the air all around me, sprinkling gently in my hair and on my shoulders. I'm a little girl released from the dark gloomy indoors, playing wildly in the light snow, laughing and laughing. I'm alive!

I venture further and walk toward the canteen which is in another building. Still wobbly from my unsteady gait, it's hard to negotiate the stairs that lead into the canteen. At the door, I rest a bit. Then I go in to buy a cup of coffee. There are several tables where people can sit; all are empty except one, at which three other patients are sitting. I'm not ready to socialize with others. Instinctively I head for an empty table, but a train of thought takes over: "I know I don't want to talk to anybody, I know that . . . but it's healthier if I sit with them." My thoughts direct me to the table with the other three patients. I sit there, drinking my coffee, not joining in their conversation, but still glad I decided to sit at their table.

I remember what the nurses always say: when patients are isolated and withdrawn, it's a sign of sickness. They try to get sick patients to be with others and to become busy with some activity; it's good therapy, they say. I remember these ideas and promise myself to try to interact with others, avoiding the desire to withdraw. There are many times like this one, where I force myself to sit with others, even though I have nothing to say and feel like running away.

After finishing my coffee, I walk outside again and head for the Chapel. Over the past years, the chapel has been a painful reminder of the significance of my spiritual life—and the degree to which it has become starved. Although I'm a practicing Catholic, in these two years of debilitating anxiety I pray very little and rarely get to the Chapel—I'm usually too sick even to leave the ward.

The hospital priest has not been very supportive of my efforts to strengthen my prayer life. He spends most of his time working with the staff. One time when I asked the priest if I could go to confession because I wanted to receive communion, he admonished me, "You don't even go to Mass. I shouldn't even give you absolution." He's so insensitive. I want to go to Mass every Sunday, but there are many Sundays when I can't even lift up my head, pinned down as I am by the invading terrors of my world. I don't know if the priest realizes that I understand the severity of his words. The only time you're denied absolution is if you have no remorse. And I deeply wish to attend Mass, but I'm too sick to move. All that I could muster in response to his admonition was a weak, "I do try to go . . . but I can't move sometimes."

But now, as I walk into the Chapel, I feel strong. I've come because I have to be in touch with God. Only God can make me well. The Chapel is empty. As I enter, I smell the familiar scent of lighted candles. Walking down the aisle, holding on to the pews for balance, I gaze up at the huge Crucifix hanging serenely above the altar. Kneeling in front of the Crucifix, fixing my eyes on it, I begin to pray, the words becoming audible amidst a gentle sobbing which has taken over my body.

I pray for God to help me become healthy. "I'm fighting so hard to come back to the real world, but I'm not sure I can make it." I don't pray for a quick cure, but only that all these efforts I'm making won't just fail. "This is the first time since I've been in state hospitals—nearly twenty years—that I'm really fighting for my health. And I'm really afraid that I won't make it." Any road to recovery won't be easy, and I don't ask God to make it easy. "I'll work as hard as I can . . . and I'll never give up. I only ask that my struggle to get better won't be in vain. I pray that I can leave the Castle . . . please God, I don't ever want to have to come back."

The silence of the Chapel overwhelms me. My strength is increasing. "If You help me leave this hospital, I'll never forget all I've experienced. I'll always remember the Hell I was in . . . and I'll try to use that suffering in a positive way." Then I make a vow, which to this day guides my professional life: "And if I can get out of this place, I'll commit my life to serving You. I'll serve You by trying to help those who remain in the hospitals. I don't know . . . but I'll try. I'll never forget my friends who still suffer here in the hospital."

That day in the Chapel, I make my promise and commitment, and then feel at peace, for somehow I know my prayers will be answered. I stay in the Chapel only a short time, perhaps fifteen minutes. My legs are beginning to shake, and my balance is deteriorating.

At night I speak with Miss Wendall about my plan—she too joins the treatment team. She and Dr. Baylor are the only ones who know the details of my plan and the ambitious goals I've set.

For another month, I stay on B-1, doing various jobs on the ward, and spending time walking around outdoors. Then I approach Dr. Baylor again for permission to take the next step in my evolving treatment plan. I want to leave B-1, the closed ward, for good and go on to C-1, the open ward. Before I was afraid to leave the security of the closed ward, now I seek the increased freedom of the open ward—it's one step closer to the outside world. Dr. Baylor comes through and transfers me to C-1. When I move to that open ward, most of the staff on B-1 are surprised; some are even cynical and angry. Though it's obvious that I've made progress, they don't believe it merits transfer to the open ward. They don't realize the depth of my efforts to get well; they're still not privy to my treatment plan.

After several days on the open ward, I'm feeling good . . . and bad. The progress I've made is encouraging, but I'm not yet free of the horrors which dominated my life just a short while ago and it doesn't help when I get a visit from the social worker on B-1. She tells me some of the nurses back on B-1 have set up a betting pool on when I'll have to return to their closed ward. Some give me two weeks, while others won't go beyond a week.

12. *Step-by-Step*

*T*wo months later I'm still on C-1, the open ward. I continue my work program doing various tasks on the ward and begin socializing more with other patients. C-1 signals my readiness for the next step. "Step-by-step," that's how I think about my treatment plan. The jobs I do on the ward aren't enough any more. I've got to prepare myself for a future life outside the Castle. When I begin living on the outside, I have to support myself. How can I get ready for that? That's the dilemma I present to Dr. Baylor. I already have an idea and she agrees with it. With her help I'm accepted into the rehabilitation workshop program located on the Castle grounds.

The hours at the rehabilitation workshop are from eight in the morning until four in the afternoon. After a few weeks part-time, I begin a full program—it's not easy. I'm apprehensive about being away from the ward for such long periods, and the work is physically demanding. The long hours strain my concentration and periodically I drift into a shadowy area of consciousness, where my earlier anxieties seem close at hand. My first job is lacing shoes. My fingers bleed as I pull the laces through the shoes, the leather cutting into my flesh. I'm not sure those fingers can do the job. But they harden up and I continue with the work.

Sheila, the rehabilitation counselor, shows an interest in my work. She starts talking to me, asking me about my plans.

"You know," I say to her one day, "you really shouldn't talk to me. You really shouldn't . . . because you can't help me."

Sheila looks perplexed, as I continue, "'You really can't help me anymore. People have tried to help me in the past, and I used it badly. So now, I've got to do it myself."

"I think I know what you mean, and I can respect that," Sheila responds, " . . . and I won't force anything, but if you need my help, let me know." Sheila's a wise woman. She's doing her job, trying to counsel me as one member of the rehabilitation workforce. But she sees her clients as individuals, each with different needs. Her help would have been good for others, but not for me. "I've got to start changing what I'm doing," I tell her, emphasizing my own resolve and responsibility. "I know because I've abused the help of others before."

Being at the rehabilitation workshop continues to present problems. I still have attacks of anxiety, and though I feel the world of Hell dissipate in frequency and intensity, I know it can return. And periodically it does, both on and off the job. I'm constantly on guard, and often tightly wound up in fears of my own potential fears. When my anxiety becomes too strong, I have to leave the workshop. My attendance record is spotty. But at the workshop I meet two other women who inspire me by their own behavior.

Terry and Edna, women in their early twenties, are both active, lively persons who work diligently and with enthusiasm. They both live outside, in their own homes, coming to the Castle each day to work. I'm really impressed with that. "They work all day here, and then they go home at night . . . and I stay here," I keep repeating to myself. I'm also impressed that they receive a regular paycheck, while I get only a token rehabilitation payment. They both become my good friends and encourage me to follow their path. That bolsters my intention to live on the outside. These two women also show me the importance of a positive attitude for accomplishing things. I remember my prayer in the Chapel, not to dwell on the negative experiences I've had. I feel really good about what I'm learning from these two friends.

I also notice that Terry and Edna are very regular in their attendance, staying the full day even when they aren't feeling well. And while at the workshop, they always complete their jobs. I struggle to be that way. I begin to model myself after them, sticking more to the daily routine, even though it sometimes seems impossible to go on for another minute. There continue to be many days when I'm too tired to go to work, or too scared to leave the ward. But gradually, I develop a sense that my work counts and eventually I become more dependable.

Edna and Terry become and remain unique friends, special people in my life. So does Sheila, the counselor at the rehabilitation workshop. Gradually, as I trust her more, I allow her to offer me advice. Seeing that her help doesn't take away from my own efforts at self-help, I'm more confident I can use, rather than abuse, her assistance. Soon I'm visiting these three women at their homes, and I observe more closely how a woman can be warm and loving *and* also hold down a job. Nothing in my upbringing, where women stayed home and raised the children, nor in my long stay in institutions, had given me that wonderful example.

Eight hours a day during the week I'm at the workshop. But C-1 remains my home and there too things have gotten better. Robin Stein is now head nurse on the evening shift. She's a wonderful person, who opens her heart and home to me, inviting me into her trailer home on the hospital grounds for dinners and holidays. She and her husband and three young sons make me feel special whenever I visit, a welcome addition to their family. I become a regular part of family gatherings and celebrations, rekindling some of the old feelings of joy that I had during family celebrations at cousin Lena's back in Gloucester. Robin's kids are especially affectionate, taking me into their lives without any hesitation. I become very attached to that family, and Robin becomes my closest friend.

After a few months, I'm shifted to the workshop office and begin doing clerical work. There I meet and become friendly with Becca, a former patient at the Castle, who now lives outside with her husband and children. As we grow to trust each other, we spend hours together, sharing our private thoughts and our hopes for the future. Becca is the first person I've been ready to tell about one more part of my recovery plan—I want to go to college someday. She believes in me and feels that idea is only natural. Does that ever make me feel good! I was afraid anyone I told *that* plan to would only humor me, or try to discourage me.

On weekends I receive permission to stay with Becca and her family. Becca has three children, and like children can, they break down barriers and bring me right into the family. It's not long before Becca asks me if I want to leave the Castle and live with her, until I'm ready to get a place of my own. At first, I wish she hadn't asked. "It's too soon . . . I'll fail"—negative thoughts go through my mind. I'm intimidated by her questions, unsure of my ability to manage. But the possibility of living outside the Castle is so exciting, I have to say "yes." I've dreamed of this opportunity too long. My concerns evaporate. Dr. Baylor supports the move. She knows how much this opportunity means to me. And I really don't think I could have handled a "no." Dr. Baylor suggests that I continue at the workshop while living with Becca, something I already wanted to do.

Two days later, I pack my suitcase and leave the Castle for Becca's. I'm still suffering from periods of anxiety, but I leave with a sense of adventure and hope. I'm going to the outside, making further contact with the real world. That's what I've been struggling for. There were other times when I returned to the outside after a stay in the hospital, but this time is different. My life is stretching in front of me, and I'm eager to get on with it and move to the next step. And now I have friends, close friends, to support me.

At the workshop I also meet Joe. He has a way of smiling at me that makes me feel good inside. Six feet tall, with broad, lean shoulders, he towers over me, but never makes me feel small. And he's good-looking, with black, wavy hair and warm, hazel eyes. I don't know whether Joe's a patient or a staff member, but it doesn't seem to matter. I like being around him, even though I'm confused about what to do or say in his presence.

Joe, I learn later, is a former patient. He'd been sick since he was a young man, had suffered a mental breakdown and been hospitalized at the Castle, but had been released several years earlier. Once out, he finished college at Boston University with a degree in accounting and now he's the workshop's accountant. Joe's always so confident and good-natured, and especially well-groomed, wearing neat slacks and a sport jacket, with matching shirt and tie. He's well-liked at the workshop, respected for his hard work and kindness. I gradually find myself feeling the same way—and more. Whenever Joe walks into the room I stare at him. When he looks my way, I turn aside, embarrassed he's caught me staring. I try to ignore the pleasant but strange feelings churning inside me.

One day Edna comes over. She works directly under Joe. She begins to tease me gently, "Marie, what's this between you and Joe? You're always looking so intensely at each other!" I blush. I'm so embarrassed others can see what I think I've been hiding. That makes me nervous— not the old panic of being pursued by the monsters of my illness, but a pleasant tension which makes me giddy and excited. I don't know what to do next, but still look forward to seeing Joe again.

Though I can now admit to myself that I really like Joe, I try not to pay too much attention to him. I'm painfully shy around men; I've never dated a man in my life. But it's hard to ignore Joe. We work in the same office, passing by each other many times during the day. Being in such constant contact is difficult. I'm unsure of myself around him. Why do I feel so mixed up in his presence? Maybe he'll detect that I like him. That embarrasses me. At the same time I'm more and more aware that I not only like him— I'm really attracted to him.

While visiting with Becca, I tell her about Joe. "I like him but . . . but I'm afraid of getting too close." She just laughs—smiling. I tell her again that I really like him. Becca has realized all along that I'm serious. "Then why don't you invite him over here for Thanksgiving dinner?!" "Why not!" I reply firmly. "Where did that come from?" I joke and then we spend the next several hours bolstering my new-found confidence and developing an intricate strategy for how I should extend the invitation.

The next morning at work, I'm on edge. I've decided to invite Joe to Thanksgiving dinner, but I'm too shy to ask. At noontime, I find myself in the office, alone with Joe; the others have left for lunch. "What do I do now!" I think to myself, almost out loud. Then, as if on autopilot, I walk up to him, and stand before him as he sits behind his desk. I'm so nervous he can probably see my heart pounding away! My invitation is but a whisper, but he quickly responds, "Sure, I'd like to do that, I'd really like to come!" Did he really say that? I'm shocked. I can't believe it's as easy as that! That afternoon I'm on an emotional high.

Thanksgiving dinner is fun, and a good idea. Joe lives alone in Stonehill, commuting to the Castle each day. He has been divorced for many years and his two children live with their mother out of state. Joe's only other close relatives, his mother and sister, are also out of state. He really appreciates spending the holiday time with a family.

Shortly after the Christmas holidays, Becca gets sick again and has to return to the Castle. I take care of her three kids while she's away, and that's a big new responsibility for me. When she comes home again, I decide it's time to take another major step in my plan. I've been in the workshop program a full year now. Feeling stronger, I want to move out of the Castle completely and look for an apartment of my own. Dr. Baylor arranges for a one-year indefinite visit status, and with Terry's assistance, I locate a three-room apartment just outside the town of Sutton.

This move is different from the other times when I'd been placed by some agency, usually in a single room in some dingy hotel. Now everything is brighter. Now I let the light into the rooms when before I would pull curtains to keep hidden. And now there are friends around to ease my transition into the "real world" where before, lonely and unwanted, I couldn't make it. These friends are really important because there are no community resources available to help someone like me reenter the community. In fact, my coming back into the community is a rare event, quite a contrast to today where everyone's trying to get patients released from the hospitals into the community. My friends always seem to be there, preventing ordinary life tasks from building into those small crises which can add up and do you in. Whether it's a question of furnishing my apartment, or buying clothes, or filling out job applications—when I ask for help, someone is there. And now I'm living in my first very own home, probably one of the few places outside of Sutton State well-equipped with that hospital's sheets, towels, dishes and silverware. Sort of a housewarming "gift" from my friends who still work at Sutton State.

But it's very lonely at first being in a strange neighborhood. I've moved to a place far away from my relatives and the familiar shops I grew up around. Luckily there's that diner down the street. I go there all the time—at least they know me there. I hope I'll get to meet other people on the block. And soon I do.

The excitement of the move wears off and I often feel tired—and periodically, very scared. Even though I'm generally doing much better, I still have occasional attacks of anxiety. But I'm determined the attacks won't take over my life. While struggling to keep my emotional life under control, I realize my physical health isn't good. Sometimes my tiredness turns into a deep fatigue, and I begin to notice that my urine is always tinged with blood. I'm worried, but not enough to consult a doctor. I'll wait until I find someone who can become my personal physician.

Time passes. I forget the tiredness which often overtakes me. There's too much to do. I've left the rehabilitation workshop and work at Hunt Memorial Hospital in Sutton, sterilizing equipment in the central supply department. It's not the kind of job I want for my future. The vow I made in the Chapel, to dedicate my life to helping others suffering from mental illness, is as strong as ever. But this job sterilizing equipment takes me another step away from the Castle, and I'm grateful. Even though I'm living outside, I also long for the Castle, deeply missing my friends there. Sometimes I can't stop crying when I think about Miss Wendall and Dr. Baylor and my lifelong friends among the patients. I tend to remember the good parts of my stay in the Castle, and I get homesick. For me, the Castle is now a home which has been lost forever.

The pleasures of my new life are many, and they fill me, gradually releasing my deep sadness about the Castle. Sitting by my apartment window one day, I watch the children playing outdoors. The sun brings a lushness to the leaves of the big oak which dominates the yard. The children dart from the shade into the brilliant patches of sun that sprinkle the grass. Shouting joyfully, they run after each other in a chaotic game of chase. Life's brimming all around. And I feel its energy too . . . and breathing deeply, feel the beauty of the day. It's one of those times when you know it's good to be alive.

After work, I often visit. I never tire of cooking Italian food for friends in "my very own" apartment. We laugh a lot together and I grow increasingly comfortable in the real world, which has always seemed so far away. At first, all I can talk about are things that have happened at the Castle, and Terry, Edna, and Robin patiently stay within my limited range of knowledge, sharing stories about the old times on the wards or at the workshop. I'm grateful for their company; otherwise I'd be cut off from people, because I can't engage in ordinary conversation. Gradually they enter with me into areas of conversation which draw more and more on current events. I delight at the expanding topics of conversation and relish political discussions about contemporary issues.

Terry, Edna, and Robin grow in their special meaning for me. But the time spent with Joe is special in an entirely different way. He comes over for dinner almost every evening, and we begin to share our thoughts and hopes about the future—a future which, without ever saying it explicitly, always revolves around Joe and Marie being together.

Earlier on, when Joe had asked me out on our first date and had taken me to the movies, I could barely move—I was so nervous. I had no idea what to do on a date. When he leaned over to hold my hand, I was appalled and refused. Oh, I certainly wanted him to hold my hand . . . and put his arm around me, but in relationships with men I was still very much influenced by the strict rules of Ma and Pa: touching a man you weren't married to was "bad."

Gently, but patiently, Joe tried again to hold my hand, and when I continually rebuffed him, he whispered, "Don't worry, Marie . . . don't be so worried. I'd never take advantage of a girl like you."

Joe and I are made for each other—we let each other know that. Married very young and divorced soon after his two children were born, Joe's very sensitive toward my inexperience with men. Never pushing me, never grabbing at me, he patiently shows me how to trust him.

Never have I felt so comfortable and at ease with anyone, and my love for Joe deepens—physically, psychologically, and spiritually. I've never before thought about marriage. It seemed totally beyond me. Now, living with Joe Balter, as his wife, is not just a beautiful thought, but a real possibility. In any case, we talk about it a lot, almost as if it's already a fact.

My work at Hunt Hospital is only an interim job. I realize I have to get more education to achieve my goal of working with the mentally ill. With Edna and Joe's encouragement, I register for my first college course in the evening division of North Shore Community College. I have no idea if I can pass, so I decide to start at the bottom, taking a basic course in English Composition. The college is just a ten-minute walk from my apartment, but the night the teacher is to hand back the first assignment, I walk very slowly. It's taken me half an hour to get there! I can't look at the grade, and wait until I return home. An "A"! I jump around the apartment, shouting joyfully, "An 'A'! An 'A'! I guess I'm not brain-dead," I muse to myself.

At North Shore Community College, I meet Bill, a Unitarian minister teaching at the college. When he learns I want to get a college degree, he encourages me to become a full-time student. Then Linda, his wife, wants to meet me. She's a child guidance counselor who does volunteer work with patients released from the Castle. Linda wants to work with me—I guess it's unusual for a former patient from the Castle to pursue a college education. But I get angry. I don't want to meet her! I'm trying to break away from the Castle and she'll be a barrier to that goal. It takes some convincing from Bill about Linda's good intention before I relent. And I'm glad I do because she and I become good friends.

A major obstacle to becoming a full-time student is money—I have none. Linda takes me to the Massachusetts Rehabilitation Commission to request financial aid. I'm interviewed by a psychiatrist who grills me about my past mental history. When he hears how many years I'd spent at Sutton State, he's furious, "What are you doing here? Do you really think you can go to college with our money and your past record?!" He makes me feel like a criminal and refuses even to consider my application for funding. Linda meanwhile speaks with a social worker who scolds her for bringing to the Commission the financial request of someone with my mental health background. As Linda and I drive home to my apartment, we're both crying. "How can people be so cruel?" we ask each other. And we know there is no justification. I'm getting angry. By the time we reach my apartment, I'm no longer crying. I've decided: "I'm going to college—without the Commission."

The next night after class, I meet with a college counselor. For over an hour I talk with him about my past, how little I've accomplished, how hopeless I'd felt as a patient in the Castle, then stressing how much I've changed and my resolve to go further. Fortunately, the counselor is also the college financial officer. Before I leave his office I've completed a financial aid application. Several days later, I receive a work study grant. I can now attend North Shore full time.

There's lots of good news to share with my friends. But then my dear friend Robin suffers a terrible tragedy when her husband dies of a massive heart attack at the age of forty-two. It's a new feeling for me—my deep concern for another human being's suffering. Well-versed in seeking help from others, I'm now helping Robin. I do the best I can and sometimes it seems to be not enough. But we spend a lot of time together, holding each other, crying with each other—not just for Robin's dead husband, but for all the pain I had suffered while I was in the Castle which Robin tried to relieve. Left with three small children, she moves back to Texas to be closer to family. I ache at her departure more deeply than I ever have.

A year after I've moved out of Sutton State to my own apartment, my indefinite visit status expires and I'm officially discharged. It's 1966 . . . and I'm thirty-seven. Nearly twenty years have passed since my first hospital admission. I vow to work as hard as I can so that this time I won't return. And I pray. I pray with all I have for God to help and guide me in my plan.

13. *Joe*

*D*uring the summer months before I enter
North Shore Community College as a full-time student,
blood again appears in my urine. Many times while in the
Castle I had the same symptom, but the doctors there paid
little attention to it, dismissing it as a reaction to one of the
drugs I was taking. Now, when I mention the sympton to
my supervisor on the job at Hunt Hospital, she immediately sends me to a urologist. The results of his examination indicate the need for surgery. Terry is there when I
come back from the operating room. The surgeon, Dr.
Kostas, appears and we both know the outcome.

"How are you feeling, Marie?" I don't even hear Dr.
Kostas's question. I know the outcome but have to hear it
out loud. "I've found something in the surgery which I
want to talk . . . "

I interrupt him. "It's malignant," I demand, more than
ask.

"Yes," he says, "it's malignant . . . and you and I are
going to be working together for a long time."

I need to be alone. Understanding this, Terry leaves
soon after Dr. Kostas. I can't believe what I've just learned.

The timing is unfair. Here I've just started to move forward, and now I'm sick and might well be dying. "I've gone through all that tremendous battle . . . and finally achieve some semblance of sanity—and now cancer," I complain bitterly to myself.

I'm confused . . . and angry. The agony of trying to overcome my mental illness rushes towards me. The struggle, every day . . . yes, every day—and usually not seeing much progress. I cry out to God, "I don't know what You're about anymore. Why did You have me struggle for all this . . . to struggle to survive . . . if I'm going to die anyway? It doesn't make any sense." I wait for an answer I know isn't coming, and then I really pray . . . and understand—it doesn't matter that it doesn't make sense!

Crying now, my body convulses in sobs. And fear takes over, escalating beyond the fear of dying from cancer, into a morass of confusing and debilitating emotions. I guess there are still too many associations with the Castle and the many times when I lay in bed, alone and sick, feeling hopeless and driven by fear. It's a long time before the tears wash away some of that old fear of dying that plagued me in the Castle, and let me consider this new fear of dying that the diagnosis of cancer presents. Two separate but overlapping photographic images of myself are folding into one, and that one image is grounded in the reality of my present situation. I begin, with intention, to put myself back together.

Somewhere from within those tears, I make an important decision. I verbalize it to myself, giving myself further resolve and courage. "I'm well now," I begin, "but if I'm going to die from this disease, I just want to die as a whole person, not someone who's given up. No matter how much time is left, I just can't stand still . . . I just can't go backwards. Not now, after all I've been through. Dear God . . . please help me . . . let me move ahead." My decision to go full-time to North Shore can't change, nor can my growing affection for Joe lessen. The more I think about these things, the stronger I feel.

Then I see again the terror of my situation. I have cancer—and the doctors don't know how long I'll live! Yes, I'm really afraid—I don't want to die. But I'm not hopeless and never again will be.

By fall, I'm reconciled to the fact that my cancer of the bladder will inevitably affect my college schedule. And my persistent optimism doesn't blind me to the possibility that cancer might even end my life before I graduate. If that's how it's to be, it still won't stop me! Encouraged by my friends, and especially by Joe, I undergo surgery at the beginning of my first semester of college to remove the tumor. Three weeks later, hopeful that Dr. Kostas has removed all of the malignancy, I'm back in my apartment, preparing for classes, determined to catch up with the month of work I've missed.

My first year at North Shore Community College is an exciting, often overwhelming challenge. Attending classes full time, working at different jobs as part of my work-study program, and spending time with Joe, Edna, Tracy, and Linda occupies nearly all of my hours. Punctuating this full schedule are the cystoscopies performed every three months at Hunt Hopsital to note the condition of my bladder. These are times of intense anxiety. The instrument used to view my bladder allows Dr. Kostas to tell if cancerous growths are recurring. Lying on the examining table, trying to remain calm while the technicians perform this test, requires every bit of control I can muster. Despite my efforts, anxiety inevitably overwhelms me midway through the procedure, reducing me to a nervous wreck before the test ends. Once I learn the results are negative, however, my whole life comes back into focus, and I leave the hospital grateful to be alive, eager to return to my schedule.

My struggle to learn how to live in the community—that "real world" I so yearned to touch while still in the Castle—continues. I understand that I've got to end my dependency on the Castle, and cut what feels like an umbilical cord connecting me to that place. But every step I take in that direction is difficult. Part of me is desperately anxious to continue seeing therapists, according to the arrangement that I've worked out with the staff at Sutton State. I would want to see someone every day of the week, but I know how harmful such a connection would be. Gradually, I terminate my therapy contacts. One of the counselors makes termination especially hard because he insists that my leaving is a sign of the failure of treatment. But I know termination is a sign of my growing strength and a necessary step. Later on, I see how often therapists keep patients coming to them, not so much for the benefit of the patients but to satisfy the therapists' need to help—and because of their own inability to recognize the clients' actual independence.

The strings that draw me back to the Sutton State Hospital system seem to be everywhere. When I refuse to attend the Sutton State drop-in center at a nearby Unitarian Church, some people think I'm being snobby, refusing to associate with other former mental health patients. But that isn't my intention. I like the idea of such a center, but I need to spend time with people like Edna and Terry in order to build my new life. These women, though more than ten years younger than me, have so much to teach.

They're always going to parties, and though I don't go, I love having dinner with them at my apartment and then watching them get ready to go out. From them, I sense what fun life can be and how to prepare myself for happy times. The three of us often take weekend trips together or go to the movies or for long walks. Each time with them is like another college course, as I learn social skills I've never been exposed to before.

There's a bittersweet side too. Since I'm broke almost all the time, I can't pay my fair share of the costs of these activities. Christmas is especially painful. I give what gifts I can afford—but they seem so small in comparison to what I get. I know my gifts are appreciated. Still, I yearn for some financial stability.

My homesickness for the Castle remains. It's the only home I've known for nearly twenty years! Sitting alone in my apartment, I remember the good times and friendships. I feel an urge to run back, to become part of that world again. There's never a time when I drive by the hospital that I don't experience a profound sense of loss. If not for my involvement with North Shore Community College, I'm not sure I could withstand the temptation to return.

The college propels me in the other direction, away from the Castle, enabling me to see that place more realistically. I miss the Castle, but more and more, I don't want to—and can't—return. North Shore opens doors for me. There are so many new people to meet. Although the students are nearly all at least ten to fifteen years younger than I am, I really like being around them. So much about the college stimulates me. I study hard, aspiring to be a top student, but value my relationships with the other students as equally important. I'm always asking my new class-mates questions, listening to their answers, caring about their problems and successes. And I laugh—a lot. These kids bring out the best in me! By the middle of my first semester, I already feel a part of student life. Whenever I go to the cafeteria, there's always someone to sit with and talk to. I'm reaching out to people—and they reciprocate.

Not all the students I meet are eighteen years old. When I'm introduced to Lois Fuller, we immediately hit it off. Like me, in her mid-thirties, she's the first friend I've made beyond the umbrella of the mental health system. Edna, Terry, Linda, and of course, Joe remain a crucial part of my life, but to them, at the beginning at least, I've been Marie Bartello, mental patient at Sutton. But to Lois, I'm Marie Bartello, college student. And I love the way I look in her eyes. We work together, helping each other with assignments, reading each other's papers.

North Shore is a small, new community college, committed to treating every student as important. The professors really care about their students and spend a lot of time with us. This atmosphere is just what I need. I feel encouraged in my courses, especially in my psychology course, which is so intriguing. There I learn about a field I've been a part of without really knowing it. I ask a lot of questions of my psychology professor, and fortunately, he's one of the most giving and sensitive of my teachers.

The world has changed so much in the twenty years I've been away. This is 1968. John and Robert Kennedy and Martin Luther King had been assassinated; there were riots and demonstrations—all while I was in the hospital, caught in a mental standstill. The impact of these monumental happenings meant little to me then. But now I'm part of this real world, and perpetually amazed and intrigued by it. There are also changes in college life. Boys and girls walk around the campus in tee shirts and jeans, instead of the blazers and pleated skirts I remember. Their hair is long and free flowing, their language equally un-inhibited. Girls use birth control pills and have sex with their boyfriends. When they're depressed, young people take a Valium. I'm really taken aback by some of these new developments.

Because I look ten years younger than my thirty-eight years, my classmates consider me part of their generation. I'm flattered and enjoy being with them. But I'm also struggling to mature toward my chronological age. It's hard to balance my desire to remain part of the college crowd, while at the same time developing the maturity I think fits my age.

I try not to be judgmental when I see new behavior which shocks me, but the prevalent use of tranquilizers concerns me greatly. Although I'm relieved to learn that some of the anxiety I feel is also normal for other people, it bothers me to see young people become addicted to what I believe is the use of medicine as an unnecessary crutch. I'm still taking medication, but it's for those deep and life-threatening anxieties which have been labeled "psychoses." I won't take pills for what I now realize are the inevitable and ordinary anxieties of everyday life.

I'm really busy these days and generally feeling good, but my past problems have not miraculously disappeared. I often visit with Bill, who's still a professor at North Shore. He's a tremendous source of support. I describe my recurring anxiety attacks to him. For weeks at a time, I have to find a seat closest to the door, prepared to bolt out of class if and when an attack occurs. Any moment I could be thrown into a maelstrom of conflicting emotions—and everyone in the class would see that I'm out of control. Sometimes I don't go to class when my fear of spinning out of control becomes too strong. Bill gives good counsel, and together we work out ways to still the impending anxiety, for example, by thinking about my friends and all that I've accomplished so far. My fear of the continual cystoscopies further weakens me, leaving me weepy and depressed for the two weeks preceding the test. Sometimes coping becomes a day-to-day struggle just to stay in one piece and go through the motions of attending classes.

Joe Balter is a seemingly infinite source of support. So often, he alone provides the reason for carrying on. No matter what I do or what happens to me, he always seems to be behind me, urging me on, certain of my limitless abilities. On December 19, 1969, my birthday, Joe proposes marriage. I don't hesitate, even for a second. When he smiles at me or puts his arms around me and holds me tightly, it's as if everything is perfect with the world. It's a feeling I hope to keep for the rest of my life. Although there are some who think that a marriage between two former mental patients is doomed, Joe and I know better.

The following February 13, with Bill performing the nondenominational ceremony in his living room, with Linda as my maid of honor, and Joe's best friend, David Kline, as his best man, Joe and I are married. Although Joe's Jewish and I'm Catholic, the service is ideal for both of us. Bill writes the marriage ceremony, quoting from *The Prophet*. The day of the wedding, I start out on the wrong foot by being almost an hour late. Terry comes over after work to do my hair. I'm so nervous that I spend two hours drinking coffee with her in an effort to calm down. Joe's worried, thinking I've changed my mind. But the service is beautiful. I'll never forget that tall, gentle man pledging his love to me.

My marriage to Joe offers me the chance to grow up—
something I've always wished for. Marie *Balter*! My new
name means so much to me. It signifies the opportunity for
a new self to emerge. I'm determined that Joe won't have
an emotionally unstable woman for a wife. Taking care of
him, receiving his love and protection helps transform me
into the kind of woman I've always prayed to be. Joe has
two teenage children from his first marriage: Jeri, a freshman at Barnard College, and Bruce, a student at Haverhill
High School. Their presence adds a beautiful dimension to
our lives. The children are restrained at first, but before
long the four of us are learning to care for one another.
Sensitive, loving children, Jeri and Bruce enjoy coming to
our apartment for an Italian dinner or a spontaneous visit,
and they welcome me into their lives. Watching Joe growing more comfortable with his own children and eagerly
sharing their affections thrills me.

Another of our cherished relationships is with our next-
door neighbors, Kay and Louis Turlo and Lori, their two-
and-a-half-year-old daughter. Lori adds the ingredient that
blends the five of us together in a special way. To Lori, Joe
is her very best friend in the whole world—her favorite
stuffed animal is "Joe Bunny." And to Joe, Lori is a
princess made in heaven. Every Sunday morning the two
of them have a standing date for breakfast at the nearby
Friendly's restaurant. While Kay and Louis catch up on
their sleep and I read the morning paper, Joe and Lori walk
down the street, hand-in-hand, just the two of them, en-
grossed in each other's company. Joe's way of treating Lori
like an adult, nodding seriously at whatever she says, fills
the little girl with a love no one can resist. In case Joe
doesn't receive her obvious message of love, however,

Lori has other ways of telling him. As soon as she learns to write the letters of the alphabet, she fills sheets of paper with "Joe. I love you. Lori," stuffs them into envelopes and brings them to Joe. While she stands beside him, her little face filled with adoration, he opens every envelope as if it were an important piece of mail he's just found, and reads the words aloud. "How lovely," he tells his tiny admirer, kissing the top of her head when he's finished the last letter. "And you know I love you, too."

Although I don't write him daily love notes, Joe knows the depth of my love. We seem to enjoy doing everything together, so much so that being apart, when I'm not in school and he isn't at work, is nearly impossible. Whenever I stroll into Kay's for a cup of coffee, she lets me in, looks at her watch and says, "Okay, let's wait ten minutes and you know who'll be here." And, sure enough, ten minutes later, Joe walks in, missing me as much as I've missed him. Even when he walks to the nearest store to pick up a paper, I want to go, too. I can't really explain it, but I just know that being with Joe is the best thing in the whole world. Sure, we have our disagreements and down times—but the wonderful feelings of "first-love" stay with us. Whether we're in the car singing Christmas carols in the heat of summer or belting out the words of some popular song or "God Bless America," we always have such fun together. A picnic in the country, or a cup of coffee at our usual table at nearby Ted's restaurant—so many things give special pleasure when we do them together.

With Joe by my side, I'm willing to try the most difficult things—even meeting my brother, Marco, and his wife, Sarah. During my last six years in Sutton, I never saw either of them or their children. Although I no longer feel strong anger or resentment about their inability to deal with my illness, I can't imagine myself easily reestablishing contact with them. When one of my cousins invites Joe and me to an open house at her coffee shop, I hesitate, anxious about facing Marco and Sarah who I know will be there. Joe, however, insists we attend and promises to ease my discomfort. I trust his judgment and, relying on his confidence, try to reduce my own intense nervousness as we head to the open house. We're there a short while when I feel an arm envelop both Joe and me. When I look up and gaze into my brother's face, I instinctively gasp. "That's all right," Marco speaks to me in his heavy Italian accent. And, to Joe, he smiles broadly, points to me, and says, "That's my sister."

I'm overwhelmed. Never before has Marco acknowledged my being his sister. Minutes later, Marco is leading Joe and me to Sarah and the four of us chat for a long time. The rest of the party is a happy blur. Once again, Joe knows what's best for me. And I'm proud, not just of my husband, but also of myself. There's no bitterness or hate in my heart.

From that night on, my relationship with Marco deepens. The more I see of him, the fonder I grow of him. And I begin to understand how hard it is for Marco and Sarah to overcome their own limitations, their own pain and sorrow, and share mine. Now that I'm getting better, we can offer each other the special love of brother and sister.

With my dear Aunt Catherine, there are never any anxiety-producing reunions. For as long as I've known her, Aunt Catherine has been my staunchest family ally, more like a real mother to me than Ma. She's ninety-one, and she and Joe get along as if they've always been close family. Whenever possible, we drive out to Gloucester, taking

Aunt Catherine for a ride or sharing a pasta meal she's prepared just for us. One Sunday, Aunt Catherine asks us to drive her to her "baby" sister's house—Aunt Catherine's "baby" sister is ninety! It's quite a scene. Watching the two old women hug and embrace, conversing incessantly in Italian, unable to let go of one another for a second, makes us feel so proud to be in that family.

A few weeks later, Aunt Catherine suffers a stroke. Three months later, Joe and I visit her, and while he's sitting at the end of the hospital bed set up in her bedroom, holding her hand, she dies. We mourn her deeply. Joe says the queen of my family is gone. For me, my dearest ally is gone.

"But I don't think you need an ally anymore . . . you've got your own strength to rely on." Joe's words ease my pain and help me realize, once again, how far I've come.

But a dark spot remains on our life together—and it's growing. A year and a half after the original surgery to remove the malignant tumor from my bladder, my regular cystoscopy shows further evidence of malignant cells. Dr. Kostas explains the necessity of major surgery to remove a large section of my bladder, followed by urethral transplantation. Altogether, I'll be hospitalized a month. I'm so worried about the class time I'll miss that I scarcely think about the seriousness of my condition. Somehow, I'll make it through the surgery, but I dread being away from Joe and my school work for so long.

My professors at North Shore are very helpful, assigning me work to do in the hospital, allowing me to take extensions in their courses. But Joe is so anxious about me, worrying constantly about my health. During my surgery and the initial recovery period, he's strong for me. But now that I'm finally able to take care of myself, he gives in to his own excessive anxiety, falling apart so badly that he admits himself to Sutton State Hospital. I'm crushed. I watch helplessly as he returns to the place we thought he'd long since left—and even worse, as he begins to be over-medicated.

When I visit him there, it's just awful. I almost don't recognize him as my Joe. He's so listless and disheveled. I cry for him to return, and even that brings only a weak response. Finally, I gather up all my strength, and though I'm still recovering from surgery, demand his release and take him home. I vow to care for him myself. Together, we work on each other's recovery. Never again, I promise myself, will Joe require the aid of the Castle.

But my illness remains. Once I've recovered from surgery, I begin a 20-session schedule of cobalt treatments. Although the x-ray treatments themselves are essentially painless, causing only nausea and diarrhea, each one terrifies me. Lying on the table, all alone in the room, surrounded by a giant iron machine that sweeps under and around the table, pointing at me from every angle, I stare out of the room at the therapist who presses the "on" button. I struggle with all my effort to control the oppressive anxiety building inside of me. I'm flickering in and out of old feelings—I'm in the shock treatment room in the Castle and the button is being pressed. Wet with sweat, I never know which room is more fearful, though each time I try to remember the purpose of the cobalt treatment room. Seconds later, the x-ray machine whirls to a stop and I'm free from my brief terror.

I still want to carry a full load of classes. That becomes impossible. The combination of the surgery and radiation force me to drop several classes, thereby delaying my graduation from North Shore. But Dr. Kostas urges me to continue my work, assuring me that together, we'll win this battle. The next few cystoscopies show an absence of malignant tumors.

"God must be looking out for you," Dr. Kostas smiles as he gives me the good news.

"Yes, I think He is," I agree. "He sent you to heal me!"

After completing the cobalt treatments, I need a series of transurethral resections to offset the removal of a portion of my bladder. Joe remains strong and devoted during every minor procedure I undergo. For the next ten years, I'll require cystoscopies every three months. When the final cystoscopy is completed, it shows a complete remission.

In 1973, two years after major surgery, I graduate from North Shore Community College. It's taken four years instead of the two I originally expected, but that doesn't matter. Physically, I've never felt stronger, and emotionally, never happier. Joe's pride in my accomplishment is even greater than my own. With Joe, Terry, Edna, along with Linda and Bill, watching, I accept my diploma. I'm prouder of that piece of paper than I've ever been of any other accomplishment in my life.

And now on to a B.A.—I've been accepted at Salem State College! Once classes begin at Salem State, I become intensely involved with courses. No longer sick or worried about my health, I concentrate on my school work with all my energy. Particularly intriguing is the psychology course on "Theories of Personality." For hours after each class, I sit around with my professor and other interested classmates, discussing the theory presented that day.

At Salem State the level of academic work is more demanding, and the students seem into more things than at North Shore. At least they go beyond my own experiences. One afternoon I'm in the campus coffee shop, reading.

Nobody else is there. All of a sudden I smell something burning. "There's a fire somewhere!" I think, feeling the adrenalin pump into me. The door to the coffee shop is open so I assume there must be some leaves outside blowing around, which have caught fire. I go all over the place, looking for a maintenance man, or somebody else, to put out the fire. When I finally bring a maintenance man back to the site of the smoke-smell, he just looks at me, as if to say, "Are you for real?" I can't figure out why his expression is so odd. He's a little embarrassed as he tells me, "No emergency here . . . and I'm not the one who can stop those kids out there from smoking pot!"

In my second year at Salem State I make my first visit back to the Castle. A conference is being held there for all the mental health workers in the area and I'm invited to be one of the speakers. I'm really nervous—I haven't ever given a speech before a large audience and certainly not to a group of mental health professionals . . . *and* I haven't been back to the Castle since my discharge. The night before I keep working on what I'll say. What can I say? What can I offer? These questions trouble me deeply. I feel inadequate. Finally, I decide I can only talk about what I know from my own experience—I can try to tell my story of sickness and recovery.

As I walk up the Castle stairs, I'm weak and shaky. "Now I'm in for it," I think. "Here I am going to give a speech about overcoming odds . . . and I can't even make it up the stairs!" I can't remember anything much after that until my speech is finished. But I know I managed to get into the conference room!

I'm the last speaker, and as I finish talking, everyone in the audience stands up. What's happening now? They all begin clapping and many come forward, surrounding me, congratulating me, thanking me . . . and some are crying. I'm overwhelmed. I just stand there, feeling small.

There's lots of commotion. Photographers are taking pictures, and reporters try to ask questions. The new head of the hospital, someone I don't know, introduces himself and says how proud he is that I've come to speak. Miss Wendall comes up and we just cry, holding each other. Other staff come over too, and offer their thanks.

And there's Rose! She's unmistakable even though all her teeth are gone now. We embrace and share a laugh. I'm tempted to ask her if she still smells the manure, but I resist. I'm a professional now, right? But I wink at Rose and she winks back—we still understand about that manure!

One old woman is sitting in the front row. She comes up, standing quietly. I seek her out as the crowd of people around me is pushing her away.

"I have a sick daughter," she says. "Can you help her? Can I talk to you alone someday?"

I take her hands in mine. "Yes . . . sure . . . we'll talk," and I take down her name and phone number.

Feeling now too overwhelmed, I ease out of the conference room and sneak into the social services office. I know that hospital inside and out—I can get some privacy in that office. I sit quietly, trying to process all that's happened, then telephone Joe. He comes over to the Castle, joining me for dinner in the cafeteria with other conference participants. It seems like everyone wants to sit with me—to hear more of my story and to tell some of their own.

That day I see the power of my life's struggle for other people. When I read the extensive coverage of my speech in the next day's paper, I'm in further awe. And that night I pray, asking for strength to bring my story to others, and for the humility never to seek attention for my own ego-glorification.

With the help of one of my professors, I develop an internship program for myself through Salem State. As part of that I do one-to-one work with the chronically mentally ill at Sutton State Hospital. I'm really anxious about returning to the Castle, but within the structure of this carefully supervised internship program, I have enough confidence to work in the wards where I had been a patient.

As I return to those wards, I know the physical spaces intimately—the walls, the seclusion rooms, the sunporch, even the corners to which I would retreat. But I also feel distant from them, as if there's an invisible barrier keeping me apart from them. While I'm on the ward I don't think much about my experiences as a patient—I'm too busy working with the present patients. When I'm home at night, I reflect gratefully on the fact I'm no longer in the Castle, and have only fleeting memories of the specifics of my time there. There are so many other things on my mind, and I gladly and intentionally focus my energy on them.

Although my academic life is progressing far beyond my expectations, there's pain in my personal life. Despite the fact that Joe shares in the excitement of my work at Salem State College, he's not well. At the beginning, it's just a vague feeling of malaise. He isn't certain what's wrong, but doesn't feel quite right. When he finally begins to complain of chest pains, I panic and rush him to the hospital. The tests prove inconclusive, and for a brief while, Joe seems better.

In the autumn of 1976, my final year at Salem, Joe begins to retain fluid and is hospitalized with phlebitis. Even after he's discharged, he appears to be getting sicker. Some days when he's too sick to get out of bed, I crawl under the covers beside him and hold him close. "You'll be fine, honey." I say. "I'm sure of it." To myself, however, I'm saying, "Marie, you have to remember this moment . . . forever."

"No matter what happens to me," he tells me over and over again, "I want you to graduate from Salem State. I'll be so proud of you. No matter where I am." His words fill me with dread, but for his sake, I smile, kiss him, and tell him exactly what he wants to hear—of course, I'll get my B.A. degree and follow through toward my goal.

By Christmas time, Joe's so disoriented and confused, he has to be admitted to Baldpate, a local private mental hospital. While he's there, his physical condition worsens. Three days after Christmas, he begins to run a high temperature and is transferred to Haverhill Hospital. For the next few days he remains in a delirium, gripped by an excessive fever that will not break. One night while I'm sitting by his bedside, he looks worse than I've ever seen him. I know then that he's not going to be all right. My Joe is dying. I call his name over and over as he lies delirious in his bed. Suddenly, he opens his eyes, looks at me, and says, "Oh, Marie, . . . I love you . . . I love you so much." When I leave the hospital that night, I'm so frightened I call Miss Wendall, asking her to come stay with me. She arrives at my apartment an hour later. That night she asks me if I'm prepared for Joe to die. I can't answer her.

On New Year's Eve, Joe seems a shade better. His fever has lessened and his color is a bit brighter. After leaving the hospital, I go to Miss Wendall's house to welcome in the new year with her. As soon as I arrive, I call the hospital. Joe's special nurse tells me there has indeed been a slight change for the better in his condition. Elated by the news,

I lift a glass of wine and toast my husband's recovery, more full of hope than ever before.

When Miss Wendall insists I spend the night with her, I agree, call the hospital one last time and fall asleep shortly after midnight. For some unknown reason I awake at 5:00 A.M. and come out of my room to sit alone in the dark living room. Fifteen minutes later the telephone rings. It's a nurse from Haverhill Hospital—Joe had passed away at 5:00 A.M. Angry and crying, I shout at the nurse, insisting she can't be right. Joe's condition had improved the night before. He was doing better. He was going to be all right. When the nurse repeats her news that my husband has died, I slam down the phone and scream for Miss Wendall. Now I believe the phone message—Joe is gone.

Dazed and numb with pain, I go through the motions of burying my husband. Bill, who married us six and one-half years earlier, officiates. Surrounded by Joe's children, all my family members and dear friends, including nine-year-old Lori, who places a love letter on his chest, I whisper a final farewell to the only man I've ever loved.

A week after Joe's death, my final semester at Salem begins. And I have to work full-time to pay for my apartment and living expenses. Keeping so busy I hardly have time to think. I make it through my days motivated by only one thought—graduating, for Joe's sake.

Some nights, however, the pain and heartache become too much, and I lie in bed until, exhausted, I finally fall asleep. I cry all the time, and sadness and the sense of loss weaken me. But I become truly terrified when I begin to experience anxiety attacks once again—I'm not sure I can survive them. Early one evening, as I lie in bed thinking of Joe and how desperately I miss him, I feel my mind suddenly begin to spin. Remembering that hideous time in the

Castle when the spinning marked the beginning of my regression and psychotic break, I force myself upright in bed. "No, Marie!" I shout to myself, again and again. "No . . . no . . . you're not going to let this happen again. Don't panic! The anxiety will go away. Just . . . just don't panic." I keep talking to myself, meeting each rise in my anxiety with reassuring words. An hour passes and I'm still talking coherently to myself. This time, I haven't gone crazy. This time I survive.

My final months at Salem State are filled with many special moments. Wherever I go on campus, I feel surrounded by affection. One fellow student hands me a bunch of mums in honor of my last day of classes. Everyone seems so proud of me, and it's as if bits and pieces of Joe are all around me. Graduation, on June 6, 1976, is a beautiful day. Terry, Edna, Miss Wendall, and many of my cousins are there, and Robin flies in all the way from Texas. When I turn the graduation tassel to the opposite side of my cap, the whole psychology department rushes forward to shake my hand. As I stand there, beaming, looking out at the audience and catching the eyes of my loving relatives and friends, I feel blessed.

14. *Healing Work*

*D*espite the demands of my full-time job as a social worker in the Sutton State Hospital system, I spend many hours, day and night, mourning Joe. When I least expect it, after a case conference or while I'm driving home from work, the sorrow overtakes me. I'm also angry. After Joe's death, I feel tremendous hostility toward him for having left me. "How could you have abandoned me when I loved you so much?" I ask him late at night when I can't sleep and his presence sweeps over me like a thick cloud. "What did I ever do to make you do such a terrible thing to me?" When the anger grows even stronger, I actually tell myself it won't be so bad living without him. After all, I have my work. Why should I still need him? The fury dissipates when I recognize it as a natural emotion of a widow, directed at someone who has, indeed, left her alone. My guilt, however, stays longer, tearing me apart with questions like, "Couldn't I have loved him better?" or "Did I somehow make this awful thing happen to him?" or, worst of all, "Why didn't I realize how sick he was and get him better medical care sooner?"

Eventually, these painful emotions lessen, and I gradually sense more clearly the meaning of our all-too-brief life together. My husband gave me confidence and experience in being an independent person, in loving others and myself. He helped me mature into a woman. How can I not be grateful for this gift? There's no denying my sense of loss—and I stop trying to do that. Unlike the other losses I've experienced in my life, with Joe's death, a part of me is gone forever. The two of us had been so close, we nearly became one.

Time is a healer and there is, of course, my work. Every week seems to offer a new opportunity to help "my people," to do something constructive for the mentally ill. After researching the subject, I become an expert on third-party payments, figuring out exactly what each patient has to do to receive his or her benefits—a crucial step toward the independence we seek for each client.

Another key phase in my work is my follow-up program, where twice a week I visit recently-released clients in their own settings. I understand how difficult the transition can be from the state hospital to the outside world, and I try to ease the trauma of this move.

As a social worker in the Sutton State system, I also work for a period back at the Castle. There's some concern that I'll be too strong an advocate for the patients, but I always stress my professional responsibilities while emphasizing that patients *do* need someone to speak on their behalf, especially someone who can understand their situation from the inside. I'm always having to assert myself as a professional and not just a former mental patient.

When I enter the ward on which I'll work, they give me a set of hospital keys. I take them nonchalantly, as if I always had those keys. Of course, they weren't that valuable to me when I was a patient in the Castle—I knew how to open all the doors with a coat hanger!

My work in the Castle is rewarding, but difficult. What I have to offer isn't always appreciated.

My first day of work, Harriet, one of the patients, comes up to me. We had been together on the ward when I was there as a patient.

"Oh, Marie . . . I remember you! I remember . . . " Harriet moves closer to my face as she speaks. "You were on that first bed for so long . . . and now look at you. How'd you do it? How'd you get out?"

"Harriet, it's good to see you. Yeah, it feels good to be back . . . and now to have a job here. But, you know, it's a lot of hard work to get better . . . and you've got to decide that you want to first."

Harriet turns around and walks away. Maybe she can't hear what I say . . . or doesn't want to.

Rarely do I talk about my past while working in the Castle, except for the time I'm asked to speak with the entire second shift of nurses. They want to know what the patients are feeling. I talk about the little things that make a patient feel good or bad, like when a patient sees the nurses go into their room to smoke or have lunch and he or she comes to the door and is told to get away—the patient feels really bad then, a little guilty or ashamed to be there. I also speak of the intense suffering patients experience, and ask the nurses not to forget that suffering even though they get so used to it.

Finally, a nurse asks me, "Do you think that everybody can get better?"

"It's not up to us to decide if they can or can't," I respond. "Just give everybody the chance to get better and then let them go at their own pace. And we have to be positive—supporting their desire to live better and not always insisting on their productivity as a measure of their success."

I feel good about sharing my own understanding and experience. At least the nurse who asked that question is listening.

My involvement with the mental health field expands, and I become engaged in a number of activities beyond my job. Armed with a beeper, I volunteer as a member of the local Crisis Mobile Outreach team. I'm on twenty-four-hour duty to switchboards that receive calls from potential suicides and others experiencing a mental health crisis. I also serve on several local mental health committees. Whenever possible, I accept speaking engagements, talking frequently to mental health groups, not just about my experiences, but about my dreams for future mental health programs.

Even with this demanding work load, I'm still lonely. I turn increasingly to Edna for companionship. Since I met her eight years ago, she has always been someone special. After Joe's death, our friendship grows even more precious. We seem to understand so much about each other. Most important, we share our strong sense of religion, our profound belief in God. Although there was little Joe and I didn't share, religion was not an issue we commonly discussed. But with Edna I can sit for hours, speaking about faith in a loving God who has never forgotten me. As a person who has recently rediscovered her religion, Edna is equally committed in her faith.

Not all of our time together is filled with heavy conversation. We often simply relax, enjoying each other's company. On sunny days, we meet for our lunch hour, eating our sandwiches by the pond, watching the ducks and birds around us. Edna identifies with the ducks and talks about how pleasant it would be to float gracefully across the water. To me, the birds are the envied species, flying through the air, soaring above the clouds. On weekends Edna always manages to find something interesting and fun to do, perhaps a drive to visit the mansions at Newport or a leisurely trip through the White Mountains of New Hampshire. We're always confiding in each other about our dreams for the future. For Edna, it's to earn a B.A. degree in accounting and become a Certified Public Accountant. Taking courses in the evenings at North Shore, she's already working toward her goal. For me, the dream is implementing new, humane programs for the mentally ill. Because Edna knew Joe even longer than I had and loved him dearly, we share that as well, telling each other little stories that typified him.

Several months after Joe's death, Edna helps me move out of my apartment. It's filled with memories that leave me weepy and depressed; also the rent has increased so that I can't afford it anymore. I learn about another less expensive apartment in a large house in a rural area. My new apartment is beautiful, with a fireplace and stunning views of the countryside.

The change of environment helps, bolstering my spirits. In fact, I'm so energized that I decide to throw a party— my first one ever—to thank all my friends. Since I can use the entire house for my celebration, I invite all the people who've helped me over the years. More than one hundred people show up. I'm ecstatic! I really enjoy being a hostess, putting out different dishes people bring. This limited budget party is a potluck of sorts. Bill is in charge of parking the cars and gets a taste of a possible future as a parking attendant, or at least that's what Linda thinks.

It feels so good to be with those who've supported me . . . and so good to give them a little something in return. The enormous cake I order is decorated with the words: "Thank You All My Friends." As I visit with different people at the party, those words come to me, again and again. It's their party.

There's a lot of crying that night—for joy, for gratitude, for memories of difficult times shared. And there's a lot of laughter. After most of the guests have left, a few of us stay on, talking more. Elizabeth, one of my friends, decides to do some psychic work, encouraging someone to travel back to her past lives. Elizabeth is into these things and picks Dottie, who used to be a student nurse at the Castle, as her subject. Dottie's husband had gone home already. So here we are . . . with Dottie going back into one of her prior lives. At nearly one A.M. she's in the time of the Apostles, telling us about seeing Peter, then Andrew and St. Mark. Then Dottie's husband calls, concerned that she hasn't come home yet. What can I say? "Oh, Dottie's busy right now visiting with St. Mark." No way! The husband's never heard of this psychic past-lives business and isn't one of your more progressive types, so I tell him that Dottie's in the bathroom and can't come to the phone. About an hour later, he calls again. This time Dottie is in a prior life in Egypt, about to go into a pyramid. "Sorry, she's busy now. She's in the bathroom," I tell him, laughter nearly taking over my words. We go on until three in the morning, and he calls several more times. He must have really wondered how his wife can always be in the bathroom, but I can't imagine telling him she's busy walking around in Egypt or Jerusalem.

Edna has become my dearest friend. Just before Joe died, she had a mastectomy to remove a malignant tumor. She's convinced her bout with cancer is over, and like me, that she's won that battle. Now a year later another tumor appears, requiring a second mastectomy, and I worry frantically about her prognosis. Still, Edna refuses to become despondent, convinced she'll eventually lick this disease. Months later, further disease materializes in her bones, causing her enormous suffering, making her every movement a struggle. Despite her pain, she perseveres. She continues with her classes, clinging to her seat, though riddled with pain. Adamant about not accepting disability benefits, she keeps functioning until her death is imminent. Only then does she enter Salem Hospital, where, relying on me and a psychiatric counselor from the hospital, she comes to terms with the end of her struggle. Her belief in God fills her with a strength and peace that makes her death a moment of beauty. Seeing her courage, both in living with her disease and in dying with her faith intact, inspires me deeply.

Edna's death, three years after Joe's, leaves me aching again. Another irreplaceable part of me has died. Only when I realize how her gift of courage has enriched my life can I deal with her death in a positive manner and renew my conviction to carry on with my work. From then on, Edna's memory mingles closely with Joe's. Never do I pray for Joe without mentioning her also.

One final loss that I suffer the same year is the death of my brother Marco. After Joe's death, Marco and I had grown even closer. He showed his affection for me in small, touching ways. Recognizing that he and I shared much of the same upbringing and that he, too, had been a victim of our father's relentless domination, I forgave and loved him all the more. Understanding our sibling relationship helps me see how much I've grown, and I'm able to be more objective about my early family life.

Despite being satisfied with my work, I feel a compelling need to make a major change in my life. The pain of Joe's death, followed by the loss of Edna and Marco, often weighs me down. I wonder if a move, somewhere far away, might be a healthy step. I'm also in a bad way financially—it's more and more difficult to survive on my social worker's salary. I need a master's degree to improve my earning capacity but with my present salary I can't afford the expense of graduate school. After a great deal of thought, I decide to move to Corpus Christi, Texas, to be near my close friend, Robin. This move won't be permanent—but it seems a positive way to make a new start.

Robin's loving encouragement during the months of job-hunting keeps me going—there are many low moments when I believe it was a mistake to come to Texas and begin doubting my self-worth. But after spending six months living with Robin and her two teenage sons, I finally find both an apartment and a job counseling Mexican-American adolescents.

Even though the job is not in my field of expertise, it's challenging. I manage to save a small amount from my weekly paycheck, and I begin to have a group of friends in Corpus Christi.

After a year, I seek to make another change, exploring the possibilities of a more holistic approach to mental health. I want to deal with both the spiritual and emotional makeup of a patient and decide to pursue a master's degree in Pastoral Counseling, thinking of perhaps working as a chaplain in a mental hospital.

After carefully studying the various graduate programs available, I apply to a religious college in San Antonio and am accepted into their Master of Divinity studies. Negotiating a loan from a bank in Corpus Christi, I give up my job and move to San Antonio, planning to live on campus and attend the two-year program as a full-time student. I arrive at the college on a Friday and spend the weekend settling into the dormitory, feeling more confident than ever that I've made the right decision.

On Monday, I go to register—they won't let me register! "Go see the Dean," I'm told.

"One of your letters of recommendation has just come in," the Dean begins somberly, "and it's a good letter. You've worked so hard . . . but being a mental patient, well, that makes it impossible for you to register as a student at our college."

I'm not sure I hear the Dean correctly, so I ask him to explain what he's just said.

"You'll have to leave. Our policy doesn't allow us to accept students with your background."

I'm shocked and urge him to reconsider, pleading my case. I go on and on about all that I've done since my time in the Castle—my marriage, my school studies, my jobs, my mental health work. "I'm not a mental patient. That was in my past."

But no matter what I say, he politely, but firmly, refuses. "We know how much you've accomplished, but . . . it's our policy," he keeps repeating. "What you've done is wonderful, but I can't change my mind."

"How long can I stay?" I ask, truly frightened.

"One day."

That's the end! I've just given up my job and apartment and I have no money. I'm really scared now—and angry and frustrated and confused. I've never been denied access to anything before just because I'd been a patient. And here is the church denying me—and without any good reason! What are they were afraid of, that maybe I'll go crazy right in the middle of a class? I'm distraught thinking about how irrational their prejudice is.

Within an hour, I'm on the highway, driving back to Corpus Christi. The only comfort I can feel is to realize that this brutal discrimination is the work of human beings, not God's will. God's teachings are right, but some of the teachers have lost their way.

Although Robin tries to convince me to move back into her house, I have to be alone. Knowing how much Robin believes in me, how badly she wants me to make something out of my life, I almost feel sorrier for her than for myself. I rent a single room and force myself to sit quietly and contemplate my future. After deciding that the best thing would be to get back my old job in Corpus Christi and not make any more drastic changes in my life for a while, I learn that the job is no longer available. I return to my room, weeping bitterly. I pray to God, begging him for guidance. My answer comes soon: I have to return home to Massachusetts.

It isn't easy saying goodbye again to Robin and my new friends in Corpus Christi. I drive to Massachusetts as quickly as I can, arriving at Linda and Bill's house three days later. When I come in, they embrace me warmly. I have no idea about the future, but I know I've made the right decision to return—I trust God will help.

Less than a week after I return, I have a new job, once again working with adolescents. I'm still hoping for work in my area of expertise, with the adult mentally ill, but this new job is appealing. Since I'll be working in a residential program for adolescents with behavioral problems—street kids in trouble with the police—I'll live on the facility's campus. This seems an excellent way to immerse myself quickly in my new job; it also spares me the difficulty of setting up yet another apartment.

Driving to see my new quarters, I'm optimistic and enthusiastic. That changes fast! My room is the bottom of the pits, a paint-spattered gloomy cubicle. Its window panes, painted a dark brown, offer me no chance to look outside. The only furniture in the room is a mattress resting on the floor. It reminds me too much of the hospital rooms I've seen enough of.

I make the room more livable. Using cardboard boxes to store my clothes and scraping paint off the windows, I can sleep all right and can then focus on settling into the routines of my new job. Unfortunately, the room's the only part of that job that I can make bearable. I'm just not equipped to work with troubled adolescents. For starters, I can't handle their foul language and tough mannerisms. No matter how hard I try to adjust to their attitudes and problems, I feel incompetent and ineffective. Six months after starting with the adolescent program, I get a new job as Residential Director at the Northeastern Family Institute, a private multi-purpose mental health facility. It's there that I can work in my area—with adults suffering from mental illness—and begin developing programs I've only dreamed of before.

15. *Harvard*

*P*aul teaches us a lot—even though he doesn't talk. We're starting a residential program at the Northeastern Family Institute for adult mental patients who have been released from the hospital. It's something like a halfway home. We're trying to prove the value of a community context for prevention and treatment. Almost instinctively, we've selected "good" patients for our program—patients who are good risks for living on the outside, motivated persons well on the way to recovery. Not surprisingly, our program is doing pretty well. But I think we've stacked the deck.

Then I hear about Paul. He's on the Castle's back ward chronic care unit, but is still recommended to our program. I ask Barbara Thompson, one of our staff, if she knows him.

"Paul," she replies, "is not functioning very well—he can barely take care of himself. But he isn't violent . . . and I like him!"

That's all I have to hear—she likes him. The next day, I go to the hospital to find Paul.

When I see him, I recognize his situation—he looks just like those patients I'd seen in the years I was on the back wards. Paul's a big, heavy guy who's really unkempt. His shirt has lost most of its buttons, but it's doubtful whether it could have covered up his protruding belly even in its original days. When he walks he has to grab the waist of his pants because they droop around his body.

Paul's sitting on a bench, slouched forward into his blank stare. I go over to him.

"Are you Paul Hodges?" I ask.

He just looks up at me and nods, ever so slightly.

"Oh, hi, Paul," I greet him cheerfully. "You don't know me yet. I'm Marie Balter . . . but you can call me Marie. I'm not like the nurses here, so you don't have to call me Mrs. Balter."

Paul shows no visible response.

"I'm a friend," I continue. "I come here to get people out . . . not keep them in."

I can't tell if he understands what I'm saying but I feel I have to carry on. "You just sit there a lot . . . and most people think you don't know what's going on . . . but I think you do."

"Have you heard about our program, The Lodgings House?" I ask. "It's a new residential program in this area." I'm sure many patients in the hospital know about our program, and probably Paul has picked up on it.

He nods his head.

"Well, some people tell me you'd be a good person for our program. We're trying to make it a real home. Would you like to come with us? . . . would you like to come and live in our new home? It'll be yours too."

Paul looks up and nods his head, "yes."

"Paul," my voice lowers, and I lean toward him, "you be real good and don't mess up here in the hospital and you know . . . by the end of the week we'll see about getting you out. Now remember, don't mess up . . . because some people here aren't going to be happy about your going to our residential home. They'll be looking for excuses to stop you from leaving the hospital. And you and I know that sometimes people don't know what's good for us—even when they want to help us."

"Uh huh, uh huh," is all Paul grunts. He understands.

I'm going on my instinct with Paul. The guy isn't even talking. I didn't know how much he was picking up on until he made those few sounds and nodded. But he doesn't have that faraway look you see in so many chronic patients. Paul looks in contact with me but he also looks as if he's lost everything in life, as if all he has left is the world of the back ward.

There's a lot of controversy about getting Paul out. "Why take Paul?" the head nurse argues. "He'll be back in a week. You can't do anything with him. Take another patient you can work with."

But we believe in Paul despite the fog of listless silence that surrounds him. The doctor signs his release papers over the weekend when the opposing nurses aren't there, and we whisk him out.

What a sight Paul is when he comes to our program! He's holding up his pants with one hand and holding his extra shirt in a brown paper bag in the other hand. That extra shirt is all he has—plus the paper bag!

We manipulate the budget a bit and release money to buy Paul some clothes and a few other essentials. We go to a big man's shop, avoiding the shopping mall because it overwhelms him.

The next day when I come on duty at our residence home, the counselor who's coming off duty approaches me.

"Marie, I think we're gonna have a problem with Paul," she says, her voice pleading for help. "I don't know if he's gonna make it here in the home. He eats with his hands, no silverware, only his hands. We tried to get him to use silverware, but . . . "

"Is that right?" I respond, not surprised, but showing it in order to sympathize with the counselor. "Let me take care of Paul."

I call for Paul and he comes downstairs, still holding his pants up. I ask him a bit about how he's feeling and how he's doing. No particular response, but I know he's listening.

"Paul," I continue, "our counselor tells me you were eating with your hands yesterday. Paul, you know we like you . . . we like you a lot! Everybody's real glad you're here. But, you know, we really don't want to eat with you if you can't use silverware. If you keep eating with your hands, you'll have to eat alone in the kitchen . . . and I don't think you want that. Now you come into the dining room with us for supper and eat right . . . I know you can do it."

We all sit down for supper—myself, another staff member, Paul, and the five other residents. I don't really know what will happen. Paul doesn't speak so you can't be totally sure. Maybe I've blown the thing; maybe Paul isn't ready for our residential program.

Watching Paul, not staring, but watching, I wait to see what he'll do. Well, he picks up his fork and begins to eat. He grunts for somebody to pass him the mashed potatoes. I'm thrilled. Can you imagine being so excited when someone grunts for a dish of mashed potatoes?

Paul is never a problem for us. He's not a "problem," but a person who's suffered a lot and been very disturbed.

He's seeking some peace and comfort in his life. He does things which some people consider "strange," and many thoughtlessly label as "crazy." But we always try to see the humanity and humor of Paul's efforts at making his place in the world and resist labeling him or his behavior as "crazy."

Soon after Paul comes to our residential program he begins a day treatment program like all our other residents. After a few days there, we receive a complaint from a day program staff member, "Paul hits people. We don't think he can continue in the day treatment."

"That's funny," I respond. "Nobody here at the residence ever says anything about his hitting people."

"Yeah, he goes and taps people," the staff member adds.

Now I get the picture. That night I talk with Paul. "Hey, Paul, I spoke with someone from the day treatment program. They complained you hit people. I don't think they understand you. I think I know what you're doing—you're touching people because you like them and want to say hello . . . I don't think you're hitting people—you're talking to them."

Paul says nothing but his face shows that I've understood his struggle to communicate at the day treatment center.

"They're stupid over there at the center," I go on. "They don't understand you're trying to say hello. Well, maybe you can change that way of touching people because it makes them nervous. They'll understand, but for now . . . it's probably best to stop touching others."

Paul doesn't answer. He still isn't talking. He just stops touching others—he never actually "hit" anyone. Paul never hurt anybody. He'd go by a person and all of a sudden tap them. They called it "hitting," but all he's doing is reaching out to others. With time, persons at the day treatment center learn more about Paul and grow to appreciate his longing for, and inexperience in communication—and they help him contact others more effectively.

But the mental health bureaucracy continues to roll on, sometimes rolling over its clients.

One day I get a call from another staff member at the day treatment center, "Paul's suspended for two days."

"He is?" I'm upset, not wanting to believe what I've heard, not really believing it.

"But Paul's been at your center for a year," I say, "and there's never been a problem since that misunderstanding about his touching others. Why is he suspended?"

"He stole a pickle," the voice intones from the other end.

"He what? You must be kidding!" I can't believe I'm talking to a mental health professional. "You're kidding me, aren't you?"

"No."

"How do you *steal* a pickle! It doesn't sound right. You don't kick a person out of a program for stealing a pickle. That's crazy!"

"Well, Paul was cleaning out the refrigerator here at the center," the staff member responds with professional seriousness, "and there was a jar with one pickle left in it. He opened the jar and ate the pickle and threw away the jar." The staff member pauses and with somber tone says, "They're not supposed to eat food out of the refrigerator without asking."

"Listen," I say, holding my temper, because the situation is too ridiculous, "I think you're all crazy over there. You want to suspend Paul for two days? Fine. We'll keep him here in the residence. But you know . . . this is really silly. I can't believe you people are for real. You know, every time I clean my refrigerator, if there's a jar with a little bit of food, I don't keep the jar. I just eat the food and throw away the jar. I would have eaten that one pickle and thrown away the jar—just like Paul did! And I bet you people would have done the same thing. I'd give Paul credit for being normal . . . that's one of the most normal things he's done!"

Well, Paul comes back to the residence. You can't undermine another agency so we support the suspension. But I say to him, "I know you got suspended, but don't pay any attention to that. Stay here for two days and then go back. Let's not even talk about it . . . the suspension is too stupid. You did what all of us would have done—you were just cleaning up the refrigerator!"

Paul continues to do all right. He moves out of our residence into semi-independent housing. There he's more on his own—doing his own banking and laundry, and cooking with a group of people. Paul's emergence from the hospital is no miracle, nor is he "fully recovered." He's just a person trying to make sense of his predicament, enjoying the small successes in his adaptation—the way any of us would!

There are others like Paul. The dilemma of each is different, but their poignant need for help is the same. As I continue to work at the Northeastern Family Institute developing post-hospitalization programs for such people, my concerns about the mental health system become deeper and more articulate. I already had many questions about the system from my experiences as a patient in that system. Now these questions are raised again, and more sharply, through my work as a professional in that same system.

I really have to question whether the mental health profession is meant to help people or just maintain the system.

How many of its workers care deeply about individuals and their special hurts? How many look with hope at individuals who are labeled "hopeless" and take risks to provide them with care? Paul calls out for us to meet him as a person, to see the beauty in his nature, and really care for him, despite the fact that for a long time he was lost in the system, a back ward patient whose chronic depression made him practically anonymous. Paul's case is not only a success story, it's a "success despite professional treatment" story.

Not that nonprofessionals are always more helpful. There are many meetings held to explain our community-based programs and seek the support of the neighborhood people. At a meeting in the town of Sutton the neighbors of one of our proposed half-way houses gather to "discuss" the possible location of the house in their area. The debate proceeds in classic directions: most people oppose the residential program, masking their deep-seated fear of and prejudice against the mentally ill with rationalizations about property values, the protection of "innocent" citizens, and the "discomfort" that patients might feel away from their "familiar" hospital setting.

I stand and go to the microphone. Without identifying myself as is the custom at such town meetings, I begin to speak, softly and clearly, without rancor, "I'm one of those people you fear. I was once a patient at Sutton State. Look at me. It's people like me that you're avoiding. We are who you fear . . . but we are just people."

I continue, describing my own history in the Castle to those residents in the town that has always considered the Castle an "eyesore," a place for the "crazies." Trying to be open to those unforgiving, even hostile "neighbors," I talk about mental patients as people, people who need love, people who can give love. "All I ask is for the town's understanding . . . and willingness to give the half-way house a chance to succeed." As I return to my seat, I receive a standing ovation. Many from the town subsequently come forward to help us establish the house.

It's not easy to raise questions about professional health care and still be employed within the mental health system. I'm grateful to the Northeastern Family Institute and its director, Dr. Bakal, for allowing just that. In fact, I'm hired by the Institute to question the system, especially in the area of posthospitalization after-care, and to develop innovative programs which might respond to identified inadequacies.

The very first program I develop brings about a partnership which continues to this day. At the Institute I'm joined by Barbara Thompson, an especially sensitive woman who becomes my close friend, colleague, and housemate. I first met Barbara while working as a social worker at Sutton State. She was also on the staff. It was a full year before I realized something special—Barbara is Mother Eaton's daughter. Her last name, Thompson, gave no indication of that relationship, and since I was then trying to focus on the future, I hadn't brought up my past connection to Mother Eaton.

We begin our professional collaboration by developing a residential facility for patients discharged from the Castle. Barbara, like myself, is recently widowed; we both have energy to spare with no place to go, and we direct all of it toward building the program.

Out of two floors of the local YMCA we create a residential program unlike any other in the area. Providing single rooms for every client, along with a communal kitchen and living room facilities, as well as membership in the Y, the program includes evaluations of each client and ongoing counseling. The residence receives a great deal of positive publicity in Massachusetts, which enables us to begin conducting workshops on how to develop this type of facility. With that professional collaboration, Barbara and I move toward a friendship which deepens over the years. For me it's wonderful to meet a person with whom I can share so much professionally and personally. Our deep respect and affection for each other is obvious, providing a good model of leadership and collaboration for our programs.

Despite the success of our programs, however, I'm in trouble financially. The daily meals I eat with the residents of the halfway house keep me from going hungry. My annual salary barely covers the rent of my apartment, plus my car and insurance expenses—I can't begin to repay college loans.

My financial problems come to a crisis the day I receive a bill for the excise tax on my car. I have absolutely no money in my bank account to pay it! I panic. How have I become such a fiscal disaster? Unwilling to call my friends and ask for loans, I pray for guidance.

Minutes later, I feel lighter. I call the people at City Hall and explain my situation. Instead of ignoring my pleas, the person in charge suggests I make a token payment until I'm able to pay the entire amount. Encouraged, I decide to go all the way—and pull out the graduate school brochures I've been saving for years. I need further education for my work to progress and for my financial situation to improve. Without thinking about the cost, I request applications to several schools. The necessary money will come. I'm convinced of it.

When the applications arrive, I pick out one: Harvard University. Its graduate program in Counseling and Consulting

Psychology in the School of Education offers everything I need to learn about designing community mental health programs. Setting aside tremendous apprehension about applying to that prestigious university, I complete the forms. The evening I finish the application, I head off to a Bingo game—and win the $400 jackpot. I'm really happy! Not just because I can buy several weeks' worth of groceries, but, more importantly, because I'm certain God has sent me a message. My luck is golden.

In April, 1981, I receive the incredible news—I've been accepted to Harvard! Although the psychology program I originally applied to is filled, the School of Education offers me a spot in their one-year full-time program in Administration, Planning, and Social Policy. And I can still take the psychology courses which first attracted me. Completely unaware of how I'll pay the required $13,000 for tuition and campus living expenses, I make up my mind to go, placing the problem of my tuition in God's hands. There is $78 in my checking account a week before classes begin. I've exhausted all possible means of acquiring the necessary funding. I propose a new plan to Dr. Bakal. If I continue working full time for the Institute, could he advance my salary quarterly? That sum of money, though not all I need, will cover a large portion of my expenses at Harvard. He agrees.

The year at Harvard, and living in Cambridge, is the experience of my lifetime. Living in a dormitory with students from India, Europe, Africa, and all over the United States, I wander from room to room, wondering what on earth I'm doing here with all these exceptional people. Everyone else, I soon learn, is having identical thoughts! It doesn't help me any when, during our orientation, one of the professors says, "Look to your left . . .

now look to your right. Only one of you will be left by the end of the term." It's only a joke, he assures us, but for me it raises the specter of failure. I laugh at his "joke" with the rest of my classmates, but inside I'm upset. Can I make it at Harvard? My self-confidence hasn't developed enough to put that question aside.

Being in Cambridge, surrounded by charming little shops and exciting people, is energizing, exposing me to a world of which I've never been a part. I realize that my school work will not be impossible, but it requires endless hours of reading texts and writing papers. I've never worked this hard at my studies, but this is to be my year of hope and hard work—and I put a lot of both into Harvard. Working full-time and being a full-time student is always demanding, and at Harvard even more so.

The staff at the Northeastern Family Institute does everything possible to make my hours flexible. And my classmates make time spent with them worth all the juggling. After just one month of classes, they declare me the school's unofficial counselor, hanging a sign on my door: "Psychiatric Counseling: Five Cents"—proving both my competence and unbeatably low fees. It's a role I take quite seriously, however, talking with many depressed and anxious students, including one girl I have to admit to a mental hospital. Harvard's like everywhere else as far as mental illness is concerned. It just confirms my belief that not only is there hope for every mental patient, but also that no one is automatically excluded from the devastating effects of mental illness—no matter what elite group they may belong to. The girl I admit to the hospital has everything going for her—she's an intelligent, attractive woman from a wealthy family. But she suffers from intense anxiety attacks, and one night she becomes hysterical, out of control.

She and Paul are colleagues in suffering—though they will probably never meet in the course of their daily lives.

My professors at Harvard are fascinating, but one particular teacher inspires me to work beyond my apparent limits. A man both brilliant and humble, his course teaches me enormous respect for this exceptional man, both as a teacher and as a person. It becomes essential to me that, in return for all his gifts, I offer this teacher my very best . . . and more . . . and, therefore, I push myself as hard as I can in his class.

During my stay at Harvard, I talk about my life as a mental patient with only a few of the students I've become friends with, and then only in the strictest confidence. It's not that I'm ashamed but I don't want to be known only or even primarily as a former mental patient—and I know public disclosure of my past would probably lead to that. But in that one professor's class I talk about my past and the painful process of recovery, which I insist is still in process. Somehow I feel safe in that class and trust the climate the professor has established—the other students in the class seem nonjudgmental and open to learning. I also work on a paper for him, extending over the two semesters, in which I try to analyze the meaning and consequences of my hospitalization. It's the first time I devote such an extensive effort to understanding that period of my life, and I gain some important insights. With the professor's encouragement I send a copy of the paper to a world-renowned sociologist whose research I refer to in the paper—and criticize! That's a new experience for me.

When my fellow students in the School of Education elect me Class Marshall, I'm deeply honored and surprised. And when I hear that Mother Teresa will receive an Honorary Degree from Harvard and be the Commencement

Speaker, I weep. I'm so impressed with her work . . . and now I can see her. Not yet fully aware of the extent of her influence on me, I weep again . . . and again . . . as I listen to her simple yet profoundly moving commencement speech.

On Graduation Day, many of my old dear friends, including, of course, Robin, who arrives from Corpus Christi yet one more time, celebrate the occasion with me. Although I'm the center of attention and affection that day, my thoughts are full of Joe. Even though neither one of us ever suspected that my path would someday lead to Harvard, I'm certain he knows what's happening.

For some reason, the news media is interested in me and follows me around campus on graduation day, taking pictures of my every move. Several invitations for television interviews follow. Once the media picks you up, it seems you get picked up again . . . and again. I respond to painful, probing questions . . . discussing how I'd been a mental patient for nearly twenty years, describing my periods of institutionalization. From the very beginning of my experience with the media, I learn that I have to overcome my distress in talking about my past. I don't like to dwell on things which are so painful, and I don't like the way people leap to the conclusion that I'm "crazy" when they hear about my experiences at Sutton State. But if telling my story will help in any way to improve community mental health programs, I have to live with that distress. And eventually I'm more comfortable with telling my story—but never fully at ease.

After graduating from Harvard, I continue working at the Northeastern Family Institute, focusing on alternatives to the incarceration or hospitalization of the mentally ill, programs like residential treatment centers and drop-in centers. And I give a lot of speeches to lay groups and professionals—talking about my work and my life. Gradually I'm becoming well-known in Massachusetts in the area of human services. But that doesn't prepare me for the shock of being chosen one of the 1983 recipients of the Wonder Woman Award.

As the applause sweeps through me, I cautiously mount the stage in the New York auditorium to stand among such celebrities as John Chancellor, Cicely Tyson, Lee Grant, and Judy Collins, and receive my award. The applause that begins when NBC anchorwoman, Carol Jenkins, reads my biographical sketch swells to a roar when I appear in front of the audience, and I stand there, feeling tiny, humble, and, above all, deeply grateful. The award, I hear the anchorwoman carefully explain, is for having had the courage to take risks in my life.

On that day in New York, the risks seem small and far away as I clutch my award and begin to express the thoughts which flood my mind. Above all else, I want to explain what the award means to me, how it opens the door of hope to so many people, most especially to the mentally ill whom I serve. I can't think of this honor as mine alone, but, rather, as a recognition, a validation of those people who've always been unpopular, those people who have known little more than rejection, discrimination, and isolation.

16. *A Voice for the Mentally Ill*

"Mrs. Balter, how can you advocate that seriously disturbed mental patients should be released to the community? That just makes them worse!" The woman in the front row asks a question that I've heard many times. I've just finished speaking to a mental health conference, and it's question and answer time. I try to respond with sensitivity to the woman; often in a case like this the questioner may have a sick relative who had a bad experience with an ill-prepared return to the community. Emphasizing the importance of preparation for both the patient and the community before a release is effected, I also speak to the other fear we all have that disturbed mental patients can never make it on the outside. "We have to give everybody a chance to get well," I reiterate, referring to my own apparent hopelessness.

The next question is not really a question, but an offering of faith. A rather short, heavyset woman stands up. I have an intuition—she's a former mental patient. These intuitions develop from living with patients; the institution leaves its mark on people.

"All I can say is, she's right," the stocky woman says, her voice trembling a bit. "She's right. Look at me. I just got out . . . and some of those guys said I'd never make it out. Well, here I am . . . that woman up there, what she says, is right." As awkwardly as she rose, she sits down, her speech ending abruptly.

The audience all turns toward her while she speaks and remains silent when she sits down. They've heard with their hearts.

After the Wonder Woman Award, the number of invitations to speak increases. But being a public figure is really hard for me. There are hostile and argumentative questions thrown at me because of the positions I advocate; many people aren't ready to see mental patients as people and insist they still need to be confined in mental institutions. Also, since in every talk I deal with my own illness and recovery, there is always the personal cost of dealing with past sadness and pain. But there's no other way of doing it. I vowed in the Chapel to use my life to help others who suffer, and that vow has been repeated and repeated in my prayers. My life is an offering. If I can serve as a point of hope for others, the past suffering and present discomfort are worthwhile. Also, I have to talk from my own experience—it's the only thing I really know for sure.

Being a public figure takes on a whole new meaning with the next surprise in my life. Lee Grant approaches me to do a movie of my life for television, with Marlo Thomas acting my part. This sounds like real Hollywood stuff, but with a difference. It isn't happening to one of those stars out there in movieland but to me—ordinary me.

After my initial excitement, I'm very hesitant. My prior experiences with the media are mixed, especially with the newspapers, which often seek a quick and usually superficial story. Too many times reporters and interviewers sensationalize my story, highlighting stuff about the back wards or emphasizing only the tragedies in my life. I cringe when I think of how often a story appears with a quote like "the stench of urine was all over the place" standing out in boldface. I can now sense when interviewers want to go in that direction. Before they even ask the question designed to elicit some "gory detail," I tell them my life story has many parts, good as well as bad, and it's not to be sensationalized.

But the more I talk to Lee Grant, and then eventually to Marlo Thomas, the more convinced I am to agree. These are two people with exceptional sensitivity. I trust them to offer my life to the thousands and thousands of people whom I'll never meet, but who will get to know me through the movie. "Nobody's Child," the title of the movie, thrills me. I cry as I screen the different scenes, touched by the dedicated and sensitive recreation of what I've experienced. The movie is so real—it scares me as I begin reliving parts of my past. Because it's not Marlo Thomas I see, it's me. It's as though someone had filmed me, and is now playing it back.

Only with the understanding and support of people like Barbara Thompson, who's now my housemate, can I go through the filming. And my heart goes out to Marlo. As she struggles to get inside the character of Marie Balter, she suffers some of what I felt. I feel very close to her—it's as if we're on a journey together. Marlo says we are sisters. We're sisters . . . and yet more. There is a bond between us that remains to this day, a connection so deeply intimate that I find it hard to describe. Maybe it has something to do with the fact that she lived inside my life during the filming.

"Nobody's Child" becomes an award-winning movie: the film receives the Christopher Award, Marlo receives an

Emmy, and Lee Grant becomes the first woman to receive the Director's Guild Award. The movie is something I can turn to proudly, and be glad to have a part in it. I never want my life story to be seen as entertainment. "Nobody's Child" speaks with honesty, and judging from the reactions of the many, many people who viewed it as the Sunday Night Special on CBS television, it also speaks in a voice people can hear.

With the screening of "Nobody's Child," my career in the mental health field has turned more toward public speaking. Having left the Northeastern Family Institute, I rely increasingly on these many speaking engagements as a source of income. They become my sole source of support, and though I'm able to speak to enormous numbers of people about the things I've struggled so long to implement, there are difficulties with this new role as well.

It's hard when people come up, as they so often do after one of my talks, and want to be around me or even touch me—as if I'm someone special, and just being near me will give them some of that specialness in their lives. I'm an ordinary person who has suffered a lot—and there are many who have suffered in their lives. When faced with this attention, I try to get people to see that it's their own efforts that will help them. And I always stress the importance of prayer in my life. I believe my life, with all its suffering, has been guided by Divine Providence, which has enabled me to turn that suffering into a constructive, positive force.

People are always asking for my advice on different things, not just about mental illness, the topic of my speeches. Giving these public lectures tests my sense of self—and at times I succumb to acting out of ego-gratification, playing into others' willingness to make me a unique expert. That's when prayer becomes so important. I pray for humility when I'm on the lecture circuit. I want to offer my life story *to others,* and not for the glory it reflects on me. I also pray before each lecture that I can speak with honesty, respecting each group I stand before. Though I may have given essentially the same kind of talk many times, for any one audience this is the first time they've heard it. Dreading that I could become just a performer, playing out a role in rote fashion, I pray that I can be there completely when sharing my story.

Whenever I think back to the filming of *Nobody's Child,* I'm amazed at how much I've grown. I was a small-town person who'd led a very sheltered life in a state hospital. And then through that movie, I became a public person. I felt so unprepared. Lee Grant and Marlo Thomas have been really helpful in showing me the significance of my role as a public figure, and most important, how I might have a positive impact on others' lives. They never actually sit me down and discuss these things. Instead I learn just by being with them in public, and observing them.

From Marlo I learn to have faith in myself, to trust who I am—an ordinary person with extraordinary experiences. I learn that when I'm in the public eye, the only way to be is to be myself. And that means becoming less inhibited. At first, when I appear in public, doing a TV interview or giving a lecture, I find it difficult to speak about my faith in God and really to show my love for the people I meet from the audience. But now, by just being myself, that faith and love can come out.

I think I've learned from Marlo because she's such a genuine person. The first time I see her out on her own, doing things her way, it touches me deeply. Marlo comes one day to Sutton State, to visit the patients. She moves from one patient to another, holding them, hugging them, loving them, her eyes filling with tears. I'm so moved. I can't remember when anyone else hugged them; even touching is not common. After she leaves, a patient comes up to me. "Your friend, Marlo," he says, "she's got real class. She woke me up so I wouldn't miss seeing her . . . and she woke me up so gently . . . so gently."

Marlo is a celebrity. But what I see is a person who's giving all she can to others, to her brothers and sisters. Yes, Marlo and I have met and I have grown.

Another difficult part of my new lecture career is the vague uneasiness I feel in being paid for this work. No question I need the money. And no question I work hard for it—giving these talks involves lots of travel. It's exhausting. But sometimes I ask myself, "Should I be paid to deliver a message of hope? Can hope be bought?" For me the answer is clear though the issue may never be resolved. I offer my message of hope as a gift, from me, from my years of suffering, to all who wish to hear. And I take in return what they offer me in the form of lecture fees, as a gift, from their hearts. In that spirit, after taking a modest proportion for my living expenses, I put the bulk of those fees into the Balter Institute, a nonprofit organization for the development of mental health programs, and into various local charities.

It's ironic in a way, but now that my life story has become public property, I've become increasingly devoted to my private life. Time spent with friends is spent as Marie Balter, ordinary person; I don't dwell on and rarely talk about my past. I've also become very interested in contemporary political events, especially the plight of Third and Fourth World people and their calls for humane treatment and justice. And as I feed my private life it enhances my ability to speak honestly in my public lectures. It also allows me to come closer to what seem to be my guiding principles, and most important, to my spiritual life.

Being a public figure has also enriched my private life in unusual ways. Remember Sister Nicky—who kindled that sixteen-year-old Marie Bartello's love for literature? My first true friend. For the last forty years, since I lost contact with her after leaving St. Therese's Home for Girls, I've been saying daily prayers for her. I assume she must be dead, considering her age. One day, I get a call and the next thing I know I'm in Maryland— embracing Sister Nicky, now an elderly woman, still tiny, still warm and generous. After forty years! We're together again—and we have so much to share.

Recently there's been a second reunion of the kids I grew up with when I was living with Ma and Pa—we call ourselves the "Beach Court Gang" after the old neighborhood street. What a thrill for me! It all started with a testimonial dinner given in my honor in Gloucester several years ago. Lots of the kids from my neighborhood—now, of course, grown men and women—attended and we all sat together. "Let's have a reunion of the old neighborhood," is what everyone seemed to be saying. And we follow through. These reunions are revitalizing. We talk of the "good old times," like swimming out at the dock, diving for coins as the boats came in, or celebrating the 4th of July out by the oceanfront. I remember more and more the good times I had as a child in Gloucester.

Forgiveness is more in my heart now. My childhood was filled with difficulty, with trauma, but there were also the attempts, however misguided and stunted, to give love. So much thwarted and unexpressed love occurred in my early years in Gloucester. At the reunion of the Beach Court gang, I see a woman who, I remember, was a girl I always wanted to play with—but couldn't because of Ma's restrictive policies about friends. During the reunion we visit a bit. "You know, Marie," she says with a definite sadness, "I always wanted to play with you . . . but never could. I still don't understand why I couldn't." With forgiveness, I try to explain Ma's attitudes toward my having friends in the neighborhood. At the end of the reunion, that woman says a beautiful thing to all those in attendance. She turns to me: "Thanks, Marie. The one person we weren't allowed to play with . . . is the one person who has brought us all together." She's crying . . . and so am I.

When people hear about the experimental drug program I suffered through, the one in which I was given massive dosages of Stellazine, they're shocked. They speak about the cruelty of forcing that program on me. Well, I was angry too at the time I was taking the drugs and for some time after my release from the Castle. Angry at the hospital system, and angry at Miss Wendall and Dr. Baylor for their role in initiating the program. Still, I also saw the other side: Miss Wendall and Dr. Baylor believed what they were doing would be helpful. Several years after my final discharge I largely resolved my anger, and in my heart forgave them both.

Dr. Baylor is now quite aged, and though we keep in touch with brief notes, I've never discussed that controversial drug program with her. Miss Wendall and I are in constant communication—yet we haven't ever talked about that drug program, either. Miss Wendall still "looks after me," calling me to see how I'm doing, reminding me to eat well and take care of myself. One day visiting with her, we talk on and on about things—as we usually do.

As she looks at me her expression changes. "I thought those drugs would help . . . that's why Dr. Baylor and I started that awful program . . . " She pauses, taking in my silent response—I'd already forgiven her.

I often get calls from members of my family, relatives of Ma and Pa—sometimes from the very same relatives who were so harsh and denying to me when I was growing up as a child in Gloucester. But now they're the ones in need, perhaps needing assistance in filling out a health service form, perhaps needing comfort in the throes of a terminal illness. I feel free of the burden of disappointment in them, of the anger at their earlier lack of love. We've all changed and I want to help them. They're my family. Forgiveness allows a lot of good things to happen.

I've also thought a lot about suffering and pain. People always ask me, "Do you regret the years you lost in the mental hospital? Are you angry at the unnecessary pain you suffered while in the Castle?" I guess my perspective is different. Ever since that time in the Chapel, when I vowed to use the tragedies in my life as a positive force, I try not to dwell on blame or regret. And I really believe that the suffering in my life occurs for a higher purpose, giving me strength and understanding to help others who might be in a similar situation. Those years in the Castle weren't "lost," nor were they "wasted." They were years of preparation, years of learning. They were years which enabled hope to grow from the desolate world of hopelessness.

And that preparation didn't take courage—I had no choice but to prepare because I firmly believe that was God's will. Others seem to think I'm a courageous woman, overcoming the difficulties that I have. It isn't courage that pulled me through. Courage is intentionally putting oneself in a dangerous situation. I didn't intentionally go to the

Castle in order to suffer—I wound up in that situation. Once there, realizing the depth of my suffering, I had no choice but to fight. Maybe you could say I chose to get better. With the inspiration of God, I chose.

My life is still unfolding. I try to keep growing as I grow older. There's so much still to do. I can never forget those who remain locked in the prisons of their fears, drawn into the terrors of strange sights and voices; many of them live in mental hospitals, strangers to this world. And I can never forget those who struggle to leave the mental hospital and stumble unprepared into the real world, into unwelcoming arms. They need our help; they need my help. I feel they are "my people." I was one of them, and in a way, will always be with them, and one of them. They need voices to speak on their behalf until they develop the strength to speak for themselves. I want to be one of their voices—to press for hope on behalf of the hopeless. We can never give up on a person—there's no such thing as a hopeless case. As we give a person encouragement and room to grow, he or she just might respond—especially if we give with love.

And now, as I become more involved with events in the current world situation, I see that the condition of hope-lessness can invade countries as well as people. We must work to bring hope to all those people denied the basic necessities, whether they live in poor countries or are imprisoned within the luxury of rich ones, cut off from sharing in any part of that wealth. Bringing hope to others means they must be empowered to change what is oppressive. We who now have power must give it up. This does not mean giving others power, but giving up our own power so others can take on their own.

Mother Teresa remains a guiding inspiration in my life. As she devotes herself to the hopelessly dying, I wish to dedicate my life to the hopelessly living. And as she draws her strength from God, I wish to become a servant to God's will. Recently, my spiritual life has been deepening and I feel increasingly a strength within. I realize that the story I've been telling is of a life that is being lived *through* me as an expression of God's will. There's a verse in the Old Testament which I treasure, and it's being carved deeper and deeper into my heart.

I will build an altar unto You, O God, of the broken pieces of my heart.

About the Authors

Marie Balter, Ed.M., Ph.D. (Hon.)

Marie Balter's courage, hope, and deep spiritual commitment have led not only to her recovery from a twenty year struggle with devastating mental illness but also to a distinguished career in the field of mental health. She is President of the Balter Institute, a nonprofit community mental health treatment, education, and research facility aimed at developing a sense of hope and vision for those whose lives are affected by mental illness. Marie earned her Master's degree from Harvard University and her Honorary Doctorate from Salem State College.

Richard Katz, Ph.D.

Dedicated to respecting and supporting healing efforts in a variety of contexts, Richard Katz received his B.A. from Yale University and his Ph.D. in Clinical Psychology from Harvard University. He taught at Harvard for nearly twenty years and now teaches at the Saskatchewan Indian Federated College in Saskatoon, Saskatchewan, Canada. He has worked with traditional healers and community healing systems throughout the world, and is the author of *Boiling Energy: Community Healing Among the Kalahari Kung,* Harvard University Press.